50th Anniversary Edition
CONCORDE
Supersonic Icon

BAUERNFEIND
PRESS

Front cover images images:
Spencer Wilmot (top)
Johnathan Safford (bottom)

Back cover images:
Adrian Meredith (top row; second row: right)
Air France (second row: left)
Bob Ware (second row: centre)
Vicentiu Ciorlaus (bottom)
All images except where noted: © Ingo Bauernfeind

How to watch the videos in this book:

1. Open your mobile app store (App Store, Google Play, Windows Marketplace, etc.)
2. Search for free QR code readers.
3. Simply download the QR code reader to your smartphone or tablet, open it and you are ready to go.
4. Open the QR code reader on your device.
5. Hold your device over a QR code so that it's clearly visible within your screen. Two things can happen when you correctly hold your device over a QR code:
   - The phone automatically scans the code.
   - On some readers, you have to press a button to snap a picture, not unlike the button on your smartphone camera.
6. If necessary, press the button. Your smartphone reads the code and navigates to the intended video website, which doesn't happen instantly. It may take a few seconds on most devices.
7. Watch the video by after selecting the correct resolution.

ISBN: 978 3 98159 84 1 4

1st Edition / Copyright © Bauernfeind Press 2018

Bauernfeind Press
Hingbergstrasse 86-88
45468 Mülheim an der Ruhr
Germany
Email: email@ingobauernfeind.com
www.ingobauernfeind.com
www.bauernfeindpress.com

Layout by WS WerbeService Linke, Alberichstr. 11, 76185 Karlsruhe, Germany
Cover design by WS Werbeservice Linke / Ingo Bauernfeind
Edited by Chris Cocks
Printed in Slovenia through Gorenjski Tisk Storitve, 4000, Kranj

Contents

[© Jean-Philippe Lemaire]

Foreword

by Captain John Hutchinson, British Airways (ret.)

[© Adrian Meredith]

If anyone had said to me in 1955 when I started my flying training in the Royal Air Force that just twenty-two years later I would be flying an airliner at supersonic speeds, I would have told them they were mad. Yet that is the reality of what happened to me when I was posted onto the British Airways Concorde fleet in the early summer of 1977. It illustrates perfectly the remarkable developments in aviation that took place in the twentieth century. From the Wright brothers' first successful controlled flight on 17 December 1903 to the maiden flight of the Concorde prototype on 2 March 1969 was a span of just over sixty-five years. It truly was an amazing century in which the human race seemed willing to rise to the challenges of new technologies in a way that we seem to have lost today. And I haven't even mentioned space exploration or lunar landing programmes.

Concorde was the product of a highly successful Anglo-French partnership and in terms of her performance she achieved all that the manufacturers claimed. When one considers the materials and computer technology that was available to those aerodynamicists and engineers this achievement becomes even more remarkable. The flight test programme must surely have been the most intensive of any civil airliner and it is an eloquent testimony to the risks involved that the prototype Concordes had escape hatches built into them for the crew because there was great uncertainty as to what might happen if, say, an engine failed whilst flying at Mach 2 at 60,000 feet.

The British team, headed by Sir George Edwards, had some outstanding people including, amongst many others, Sir Stanley Hooker (father of the Olympus engine), Sir Archibald Russell and Ted Talbot. My admiration for this brilliant team of boffins knows no bounds; compressibility of air at supersonic speeds presents profound challenges which were overcome by innovative and imaginative solutions. They created an aeroplane that was as beautiful to fly as she was to look at and which, in sustained supersonic flight, performed quite effortlessly. So effortlessly in fact that a friend of Sir George Edwards went on a Concorde flight in the early days and on his return home complained bitterly to Sir George about how ordinary the flight had been. To which Sir George replied: "Ah yes; that was the hard part: to make it seem so ordinary." I believe it was the architect Sir Hugh Casson who once described Concorde as a piece of twentieth-century sculpture. That defines her perfectly: she was a fusion of art and technology into a sublime and iconic whole.

I have often been asked what she was like to fly. I would say that Concorde was an immensely powerful, finely tuned and very responsive thoroughbred. Trimmed up properly, she could be flown with the use of thumb and forefinger alone. She was incredibly easy to fly. In the mid-1980s various formation flights were organized – some with the Red Arrows and one famous one when four Concordes flew in formation with each other. There was some concern about how easy it was going to be to do this from a handling aspect as well as concern about the jet wake and how that might affect other aircraft in the formation. These concerns proved groundless and it led over the years to many formations being flown with the 'Reds' whose own tribute to the magnificent Concorde was to create their own 'Concorde formation'. Having said all this, although she was very easy to fly, she was a demanding and unforgiv-

ing aeroplane to manage. If you were not on top of your game she could make a complete fool of you. If something went wrong when flying at twice the speed of sound at 60,000 feet the problem had to be dealt with effectively and decisively; it was essential that all members of the flight crew knew exactly what their roles were and had to work flat out until the problem was resolved.

The Concorde fleet was comprised of a close-knit team consisting of flight-deck crew, cabin crew, ground engineers, refuellers, check-in staff, dispatchers, flight planners, load-sheet staff and a whole host of other ground staff. Everyone involved was captivated by this beautiful aircraft and worked their socks off to make the operation the great success that it became in British Airways. It is always dangerous to cite any one group for special mention as the operation was dependent on the professionalism of everyone involved but I feel I must single out the ground engineers. They were the unsung heroes of Concorde who were very much in the background but without whose expertise and skill the aeroplane could not have flown. They were the most remarkably dedi-

cated group of people, doing a job that required real engineering skills. I would like to record my thanks and appreciation to the entire Concorde team and to all those passengers who flew on her over the years for enabling me to fly this wondrous aircraft for fifteen glorious years.

I am delighted to have been asked to write the foreword to this book because, above all else, it is a celebration of Concorde and all that she meant to those who knew her. I would like to leave you with a final thought, the story of a flight I did to Washington in 1978. I had been contacted by British Airways a few days before the flight to tell me that an elderly American woman was going to be one of my passengers and that she was a passionate lover of aeroplanes. She had been the first person to buy a ticket on United Airlines when they started up in the 1920s and had been their guest of honour at a 50th birthday celebration which had taken place a year or two before this Concorde flight. Would I please look after her? On the flight to Washington, after the meal service was over, I asked the cabin crew to bring her up onto the flight deck. Having got her installed in the jump seat, we started

to chat about her interest in aviation. Eventually I asked when she had first seen an aeroplane. Oh, she said, it was when one of the Wright brothers landed at Savannah, Georgia in 1908. Then, with some trepidation, I asked her when she had first flown. Her reply: "I first flew with Louis Blériot in 1911." My jaw must have fallen to the floor; there is no response to a comment like that. Here I was talking to a woman who had gone in her lifetime from flying with Blériot at 23 miles per hour to flying with me in a Concorde at 23 miles per minute. It humbles me to think that I have spoken to and shaken hands with someone who has spoken to and shaken hands with the Wright brothers and with Louis Blériot. It says it all about aviation in the twentieth century. She stayed up on the flight deck for the landing into Washington and announced as she got off that she was never going to fly again: now that she had flown on Concorde, the supreme achievement of passenger flight, she had done it all.

People never spoke about *the* Concorde or *a* Concorde: she was simply Concorde, the ultimate flying experience. I do hope you enjoy this book as much as I enjoyed flying the beautiful white bird.

Foreword

by Captain Béatrice Vialle, Air France

[Courtesy of Béatrice Vialle]

Flying Concorde was a dream that every pilot cherished, more or less secretly. She was the aviation flagship in both design and technology. Unrivalled to this day for her technical performance and aesthetics, she will remain for eternity a pilot's grail.

Having started my flying career, somewhat modestly, in 1984 at Air Littoral on a small turboprop aircraft called the Bandeirante, I had the opportunity – during the Cannes Film Festival and the Monaco Grand Prix – to park my plane next to the magnificent bird in Nice. Obviously, my admiration for Concorde prompted me to ask the pilots for permission to board, just to have a look. Although security rules then were far less strict than they are today, the crew declined. My disappointment was boundless.

I promised myself then, that if one day given the opportunity to fly the aircraft, I would offer such a wonderful experience to all my colleagues who wanted to see this legendary aircraft. I did this motived by the same spirit with which I agreed to contribute to this book by writing a foreword – to share my passion for this aircraft with you.

My Concorde experience was short but enormously intense. It all began in early 2000 when I was a co-pilot on the Boeing 747. Having had the good fortune of having two children, born in 1994 and 1997, after nine years as first officer on the B-727, A-320, and B-747, I had made a decision in 1994 to remain a first officer on the B-747 rather than taking up the position of captain

We regularly make career choices and obviously our first choice at the time was always Concorde. By 2000 I had therefore become a veteran co-pilot on the seniority list, which allowed me to be considered for the position of co-pilot on Concorde. To this day, I still remember the phone call from Concorde's chief pilot asking me whether I was available to do a familiarization flight on the aircraft. I always felt this dream was unachievable but I realized then that it might become a reality.

A year earlier, an urgent mission for Air France had allowed me to fly to New York on board Concorde; I was delighted that I'd be making such an unexpected flight, along with the 'happy few'. What a joy it was to have access to the aircraft, to discover its narrow cabin and even – during the flight – to be invited to the cockpit and finally admire all its very specific controls. Despite being just a spectator, I was happy already.

My Concorde conversion course began in May. What was totally new to me was to learn about flying faster than the speed of sound. It was absolutely fascinating to discover all the new phenomena encountered during supersonic flight and the complex challenges so brilliantly mastered by Concorde's engineers. After acquiring this knowledge, the simulator phase and training for the procedures of the three flight domains – subsonic, transonic and supersonic –began, as well as all the various abnormal measures that might require implementation.

Unfortunately, just after the final simulator exam, the Concorde accident occurred. We were all deeply devastated, and our course was interrupted before we had a chance to fly the aircraft. For a year, we attentively followed the progress of restoring Concorde's airworthiness certificate, which included the development of new Michelin tyres and the in-

stallation of Kevlar liners in the fuel tanks. Thanks to this elaborate modification, Concorde regained her airworthiness certificate and therefore the chance of returning to the air.

Having maintained our skills with simulator training throughout this period, we were eager to see her take off so proudly again and eventually be able to fly her. However, on 11 September 2001, I was in Châteauroux for my first hour of offline flight training (without passengers) to learn how to operate this very special aircraft, and how to take off and land. Obviously, my joy for having completed this very first flying hour at the controls of this beautiful machine was totally shattered by the tragic events in New York which again led to the question: Would Concorde ever resume her flights to New York?

A month later Concorde was to overcome this obstacle. After my four hours of offline flight, I had the opportunity to make my first Paris–New York crossing in Concorde in early October 2001. The flight remains forever etched in my memory. The workload was enormously intense. The aircraft required flawless

timing, permanent anticipation, optimal concentration and it took me all my time, until the end of the flight, to really appreciate that I had enjoyed my transatlantic crossing in Concorde.

During my Concorde years, with such access to the exceptional technological prowess of the aircraft, which made piloting such a wonderful experience, every flight was special. It says everything that the entire Concorde team – the technicians, ground crew, airline staff and air crew – was always totally committed to ensuring that each flight was as perfect as possible for the passenger. This synergistic search for perfection was so enriching and rewarding that it increased tenfold the pleasure of flying such an aircraft.

I was very happy to be able to offer my parents a return flight from New York, at my side, making this incredible and almost inaccessible experience of supersonic flight a reality for them. This was the best way for me to express my gratitude for their support during my studies and to share with them my pride.

My last flight was very moving. We were flying a supersonic loop over the Atlantic with Concorde

lovers on board. Some of them had saved a lifetime to make their dream – to fly twice the speed of sound, Mach 2 – come true. For the last time in its Air France career, I landed the almost-mythical aircraft at Roissy where a huge crowd was gathered. I feel extremely privileged, honoured and proud to have been the only female Concorde pilot at Air France.

After the end of Concorde in May 2003, another challenge awaited me: becoming captain on a Boeing 747. Therefore, the massive disappointment of Concorde's retirement opened new doors: another position with Air France, and more responsibilities for the rest of my career. First, I became a captain on the classic Boeing 747, then on the Boeing 747-400 and now on the Boeing 777.

Concorde was the result of extraordinary cooperation between France and Great Britain. Today, Airbus owes a great deal to this project that was so futuristic and daring for its time. Indeed, most of the technological innovations developed for Concorde are now standard in modern aircraft.

Concorde will forever remain an aviation legend.

A Celebration of Concorde

For more than half a century, Concorde has captured the imagination of people from all over the world. To this day, she is an extraordinary feat of engineering, as well as a unique blend of power, grace and beauty. Just as the great ocean liners once ruled the waves as symbols of French and British engineering excellence, Concorde flew the flag after first taking to the skies in 1969 - the same momentous year when Neil Armstrong and Buzz Aldrin set their feet on the moon.

Concorde was not only a technological triumph and design icon, she was an embodiment of hope and optimism in the second half of the changeful twentieth century. Concorde was one of the most ambitious technological endeavours of the 1960s, only second to the American and Soviet space programmes. Very much like the Apollo programme, Concorde suffered worrying setbacks during her development as well as a tragic accident during her operational caroor. Nevertheless, these sobering moments never derogated from the unshakeable belief of Apollo's and Concorde's fathers in their ability to overcome virtually every obstacle. As a result, Concorde proved that two proud nations, France and Britain - once centuries-long rivals - could come together to rise above technological, political, cultural, financial and language barriers to build an extraordinary aircraft that made a huge contribution in paving the way for successful international cooperation such as Airbus and the European Space Agency (ESA). Moreover, Concorde was the first aircraft to be born in two countries.

Flying with her was a thrill nobody would ever forget. With her top speed of Mach 2 or twice the speed of sound, Concorde was faster than a rifle bullet, thus traveling a mile every 2½ seconds. While flying at 60,000 feet, at the edge of space, you could see the sky turn deep blue with the view of the curvature of the earth, and enjoy superb service, champagne and a cuisine rivalling the world's best restaurants. In her spectacular career, Concorde turned heads wherever she appeared, admired by millions of enthusiasts worldwide and serving as an inspiration for future aeronautical engineers.

"She's brought cities together, brought people closer, and reminded us all that we can do extraordinary things."

British Airways

"Concorde will never really stop flying because she will live on in people's imagination."

Jean-Cyril Spinetta, former Air France chairman

Acknowledgements

Commemorating the fiftieth anniversary of her maiden flight, this volume is a celebration of Concorde, her charisma, her uniqueness, and her legacy - as told by those French and British professionals who skilfully flew her, served aboard her and kept her flying. If this work can make a contribution to keep the Concorde dream alive, I would be most grateful. To say it with the words of Concorde passenger Ben Wang: "So fasten your seatbelt, sit back, relax and let's shoot into the stratosphere!"

Ingo Bauernfeind,
Honolulu, Hawaii, 26 November 2018

(15 years to the day since Concorde made her very last flight)

Like the development and manufacture of Concorde, this book is the result of international cooperation. I am sincerely indebted to the dozens of Concorde professionals and enthusiasts who consented to be interviewed and submitted their personal experiences, recollections and personal material.

Therefore, I would like to express my special gratitude to John Hutchinson, Béatrice Viallc, Pierre Grange (APCOS), Gérard Duval, Jim Davies (British Airways Museum), Patrick Sevestre, Ian Kirby, Philip Cairns, Ricky Bastin, Adrian Meredith, Suzanne O'Donoghue, Iona Fergu-con, Annick and Claude Moyal, Nicole Méneveux, Alain Verschuere, Frank Debouck, Jean-François Louis, Alain Rolland, Katie John and Nigel Ferris (*Mach 2* magazine), Ian Dick, Richard Thomas, Johnathan Safford, Ben Wang, Bernard Charles, Jean-Philippe Lemaire, Guy Cervelle, Michel Thorigny, Aris Pappas, Caroline Cadier, and many more.

The following contributed vital information: Air France: Susanne Freitag/ f2 KREATION; Air France Museum: Jean Signoret, Bernard Pourchet. Airbus: Cassian Koshorst, Charlotte Dutilh, Hans-Ulrich Willbold, Sylvain Ramadier, Philippe Créach, Sarha Foumba and Agnes Carmes; British Airways/British Airways Museum: Gayna Fitzgerald, Barry Ballard and Howell Green; Rolls-Royce: Peter Collins.

Special thanks and gratitude go to: Musée de l'air et de l'espace, Le Bourget: Catherine LeBerre, Christophe Goutard, Alex Jolivet and Philippe Gebarowski; Technik Museum Sinsheim: Hermann Layher and Simone Lingner; Brooklands Museum Trust Ltd: Allan Winn, Julian Temple and Michelina Caliendo-Sear; *Air & Space Smithsonian* magazine: Linda Shiner; Smithsonian Institution: Dr Robert van der Linden; Aerospace Bristol: Zoe Watson; Museum of Flight, Seattle: Ted Huetter; Musée Delta, Paris: Alexandre Pozder; Manchester Airport: Runway Visitor Park; Intrepid Sea, Air & Space Museum, New York; Musée Aeroscopia, Toulouse; and British Ministry of Defence.

Many thanks also to Marcus Linke for the cover design and the desktop publishing, Matthias Nienhaus for translation, Marc Feldermann for assistance, Chris Cocks for editing, and all the photographers who have contributed to this book.

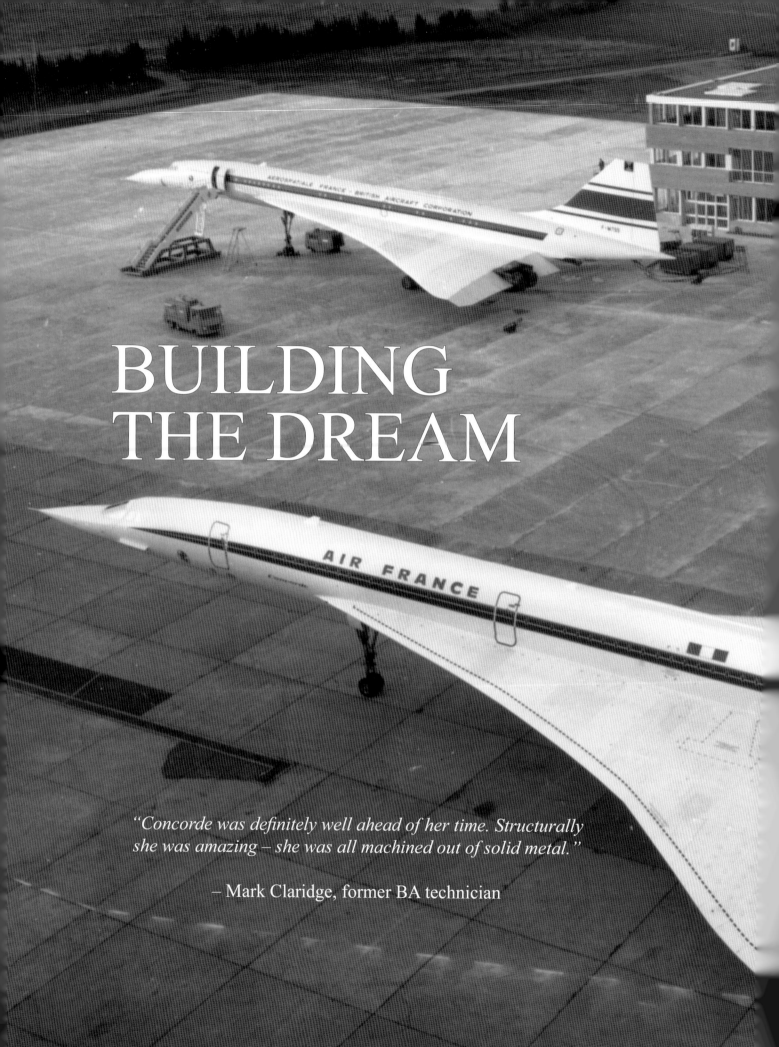

BUILDING
THE DREAM

"Concorde was definitely well ahead of her time. Structurally she was amazing – she was all machined out of solid metal."

– Mark Claridge, former BA technician

Early Studies

The German Heinkel 178 was the world's first jet-powered aircraft, taking to skies in August 1939.
[U.S. Air Force]

Take-off of Britain's first jet aircraft, the Gloster E.28/39 in May 1941.
[Royal Air Force, MOD, Crown Copyright]

The Anglo-French Concorde was the culmination of decades of aircraft design and research work conducted under war and peacetime conditions, leading to an aircraft that is still an inspiration to designers around the world. The desire to fly as fast as possible is as old as aviation itself. Since the early days, when the Wright Brothers and other pioneers took to the skies, speed has become one of the defining factors for aircraft designers and pilots – not only for prestige but also for practical reasons: saving time when travelling from one place to another has always been a human endeavour.

The history of supersonic flight can be traced back to World War II, at a time when aviation technology was making rapid advances due to the need to design more sophisticated aircraft than the enemy. Besides the construction and use of piston-powered fighters, bombers and many other aircraft types, British and German engineers developed and tested various jet and rocket engines. The world's first flight of a jet-powered aircraft took place in August 1939, when the Heinkel 178, powered by Hans von Ohain's HeS 3 turbojet engine, took to the skies. The British Gloster E.28/39 made her maiden flight in May 1941, powered by Frank Whittle's W.1, followed by the American Bell XP-59 in October 1942, built with two GE Type 1A turbojets. While propeller-driven aircraft designed prior to or during World War II could not reach speeds much beyond 450 mph (725 kph), the advent of jet and rocket technology promised flying as fast as the speed of sound - also known as supersonic speed.

Watch Video:

Genesis of Concorde

Please see instructions on page 2.

The Speed of Sound

The speed of sound is the distance a sound wave propagates through an elastic medium. At 20°C (68°F), the speed of sound is about 343 metres per second (1,235 kph, 767 mph), or a kilometre in 2.9 seconds, or a mile in 4.7 seconds.

Concorde's British Ancestry

During the war, after the tide had turned against Germany, the Luftwaffe became desperate to defend the homeland against the armadas of Allied bombers dominating the skies over Europe. As a result, advanced interceptors such as the jet-powered Messerschmitt 262 or the rocket-propelled Messerschmitt 163 were designed to counter the Allied bombing raids, the latter even capable of a speed of about 620 mph (1,000 kph). Built in small numbers and introduced late in the war, these aircraft had no impact on its outcome. At the same time, the Royal Air introduced its Gloster Meteor which was successfully used to intercept German V-1 flying bombs and whose early post-war variants were capable of reaching speeds in excess of 600 mph. Unlike Allied aircraft builders, German designers and engineers using state-of-the-art wind tunnel technology for determining the best aerodynamic shape, constructed various arrow-shaped aircraft with delta wings (named after the triangle-shaped Greek letter 'delta') and experimented with some even more radical designs. After Germany's surrender in May 1945, various operational jet- and rocket-powered fighters, bombers, prototypes and tons of blueprints for unfinished aircraft designs became war prizes for the victorious Allied powers – United States, Great Britain, and the Soviet Union – with most of them shipped to America and Britain for further testing and assessment. Moreover, numerous renowned German engineers and designers continued their careers working for U.S. and British aircraft manufacturers, and in some cases in the USSR. Two of these were the aerodynamicists Dietrich Küchemann and Johanna Weber who joined the aerodynamics department at the British Royal Aircraft Establishment in Farnborough in 1946 and who were both later naturalized as British citizens.

During the war, however, British engineers also worked on a secret jet aircraft named Miles M.52 as a response to German developments. In order to reach unheard-of speeds of 1,000 mph (1,600 kph) during level flight, it involved a very high proportion of cutting-edge aerodynamic research and innovative design work. Before test-flight stage, however, the M.52 was cancelled shortly after the end of the war due to budget cuts on military spending. It was, however, revived as a series of three unmanned rocket-powered 30-percent scale models of the original manned full-scale M.52. These unmanned scale models were air-launched from a modified de Havilland Mosquito mother ship.

After the war, British, American, and Soviet high-speed research institutions retested the Me 262 to gain experience for their own supersonic aircraft designs. Some Me 262 and Me 163 pilots claimed to have exceeded Mach 1 in straight-down dives during the war.
[U.S. Air Force]

Prototype of the rocket-powered Me 163 designed to intercept Allied bombers.
[Bundesarchiv, Photo 146-1972-058-62 / CC-BY-SA 3.0]

During the war, the design and the research gained from the original M.52 was shared with the American company Bell Aircraft which built the rocket-powered Bell X-1. On 14 October 1947, it became the first aircraft to break the sound barrier with U.S. Air Force test pilot Chuck Yeager at the controls. It was drop-launched from the bomb bay of a B-29 bomber and reached Mach 1.06 (700 mph, 1,100 kph). A year later, a radio-controlled M.52 reached Mach 1.38 (1,060 mph, 1,700 kph) after

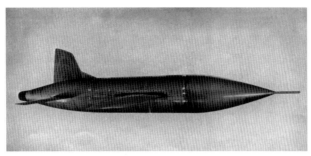

The unmanned Miles M.52 could reach Mach 1.38 but had to be air-launched from a mother ship.
[Royal Aircraft Establishment / Crown Copyright]

A de Havilland Mosquito on the ground with a Miles M.52 model in place below the fuselage.
[Royal Aircraft Establishment / Crown Copyright]

In 1947 the American pilot Chuck Yeager broke the sound barrier in his drop-launched rocket-powered Bell X-1 aircraft.
[U.S. Air Force]

In 1948 British pilot John Derry made the first supersonic flight in the jet-powered de Havilland DH 108 'Swallow' after taking off under its own power.
[U.S. Navy]

an earlier attempt prior to Chuck Yeager's historic flight had failed. However, the first supersonic flight by a jet-powered aircraft that took off under its own power and landed safely afterwards was undertaken by British pilot John Derry in a de Havilland DH 108 'Swallow' on 9 September 1948. Three of these aircraft were built and all crashed one after another, killing their pilots, among them Geoffrey de Havilland Jr in 1946, the son of the company founder. Next came a succession of various research aircraft designed to investigate the challenges of supersonic flight.

Compared to subsonic aircraft, lift is created by different means in aircraft flying supersonically. In order to attain the appropriate amount of lift without unacceptable drag, the wings have to be very short, fairly stubby, and not too long and thin. Although such a short wingspan works fine at supersonic speeds (1,350 mph and more), the trade-off is usually a lack of lift at low speed occurring during take-off and also landing.

Intense research and flight testing led to the conclusion that one of the best aerodynamic shapes for high-speed flying incorporates a delta-wing shape. Given a sufficiently large angle of rearward sweep, the delta wing's main advantage is that its front is not affected by the shock wave formed at the aircraft's nose as the aircraft

approaches and exceeds the sound barrier, thus becoming supersonic. The wing's rearward sweep enables the aircraft to fly at (high) subsonic, transonic (close to the sound barrier) or supersonic speeds. Moreover, the delta-wing shape provides the largest total wing area in order to create lift for the entire wing, thus giving the aircraft a very high overall manoeuvrability. Despite its advantages at high and supersonic speeds, the delta wing has a high drag due to its low-aspect ratio causing a significant reduction in lift at slower speeds, in particular during take-off and landing. In order to generate enough lift during these critical stages of a flight and not to crash to ground, the pilots of early delta wing aircraft were forced to take off and land at high speeds compared to conventional swept-wing aircraft. Designers and engineers at the Royal Aircraft Establishment in Farnborough tried to find a solution for this problem. Dietrich Küchemann and Johanna Weber who had been members of the team responsible for the high-speed-wing concept were concerned about the wing's drawback at low speeds. Therefore, a number of test aircraft were constructed to fully investigate this problem and modify the existing delta-wing design, the most notable of them the Handley Page 115.

Further research and wind-tunnel testing showed

The Handley Page 115 served as a testbed for low-speed research in support of the Concorde development programme.
[© Airbus]

The HP 115 was able to demonstrate rapid changes of bank, while still safely retaining control at speeds as low as 69 mph (111 kph).
[© Airbus]

The RAF Avro Vulcan bomber designed in the 1950s was a successful delta-wing design that even served as a flying testbed for Concorde's Olympus engines. An aircraft designed with a delta wing is more robust than an aircraft of similar size with swept wings, as well as having more internal space for fuel tanks in the wings.
[RAF/MOD 45133331]

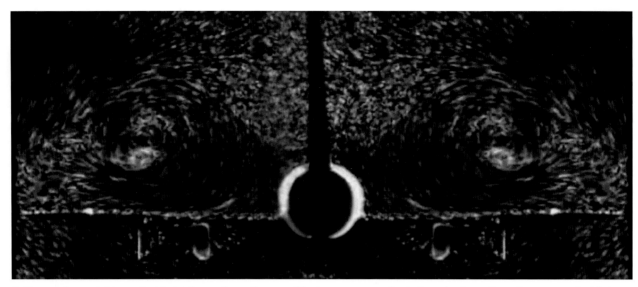

A Concorde model in a wind tunnel seen from the rear. The two masses of rotating air above the wings are called 'wing vortices'. The Office National d'Etudes et de Recherches Aérospatiales (ONERA), France's national aerospace research centre, discovered the increase of lift due to vortex at low speed and high angle of attack on the delta wing in 1951.
[© Airbus]

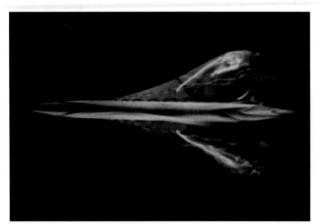

An aircraft with a delta wing running for most of the fuselage's length at a high angle of sweep is capable of a good aerodynamic performance at low speeds as well as sustaining a low drag in supersonic flight due to its relatively shorter wings which are swept back at a high angle.
[© Airbus]

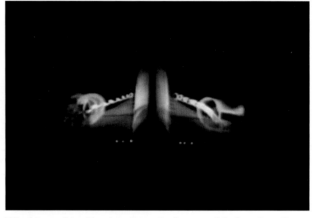

Wind tunnel testing has been indispensable for aircraft development since the early days of aviation.
[© Airbus]

that a delta wing generates large vortices over the wing at low speeds and high nose-up angles. A vortex on a wing can be described as a cone of swirling air which stretches from the wing's front to its rear. These vortices increase the speed of the air on the wing's top surface, thus significantly increasing the lift at low speeds. Küchemann and his team came to the conclusion that a larger sweep angle would result in a more robust vortex above the wing, and that a longer wing would enable the vortex to operate over a greater distance, thus creating more lift.

In 1954, the Fairey Delta 2 became the first British purpose-built supersonic research aircraft and the world's first capable of reaching Mach 1.5 (1,000 mph). Incorporating some of the research work of Küchemann's team, it demonstrated that a highly swept delta wing indeed allowed take-offs and landings at relatively low speeds by generating sufficient lift. However, in order to generate that vortex lift for safe flight operations at low speeds, the pilot had

The Fairey Delta 2 was the first aircraft fitted with a droop nose. Both prototypes are preserved in museums.
[Crown Copyright]

With a top speed of Mach 2, the English Electric Lightning provided valuable practical experience for the development of a Mach 2 airliner.
[© Airbus]

Seven Lightnings in formation flight.
[© Airbus]

A Lightning's Mach meter approaches the top speed of Mach 2.
[© Airbus]

to point the aircraft's nose significantly skyward, and was thus unable to see the runway in front of him. This posed a particular problem during landing which was solved by fitting the Fairey Delta 2 with a 'droop nose'. It could be moved down, thus enabling the pilot to see forward and down. The concept of a 'droop nose' would become one of Concorde's significant features contributing to her characteristic appearance. In 1964, two years after signing the Anglo-French contract to build Concorde, one of the two Fairey Delta 2 prototypes was modified to serve as a testbed for the development of the 'ogee delta' (S-curved) wing design. This wing was the next developmental stage for the proposed BAC Type 223, a concept for a British commercial supersonic airliner that partly formed the basis for Concorde. After the rebuilt Fairey Delta 2 had been renamed BAC/ Fairey Type 221, the successful flight testing with the ogee delta wing led subsequently to the decision to adopt it for Concorde.

Concorde's French Ancestry

While Britain was able to gain technical expertise and operational experience for the development of future military and civilian jet-powered aircraft as early as during the war, France, which would eventually become Britain's partner in designing and building Concorde, was not. Occupied by Germany since 1940, French design-ers, engineers, and pilots had to wait until national liberation following D-Day in 1944 before they could rebuild their once-proud aviation industry.

One such engineer was René Leduc who already had been experiment-ing with ramjet technolo-gy as early as the 1930s but whose work had also been interrupted by the war. A ramjet is a variant of an air-breathing jet en-gine that uses the engine's forward motion to com-press incoming air without an axial compressor or a centrifugal compressor. Unable to produce thrust at zero airspeed, ramjets cannot move an aircraft from a standstill. There-fore, a ramjet-powered air-craft requires an assisted take-off like a rocket-as-sist to accelerate it to a speed where it can begin producing thrust. Ramjets work most efficiently at supersonic speeds around Mach 3 (2,300 mph, 3,700 kph) but can operate up to speeds of Mach 6. In April 1949, the Leduc 0.10 was air-launched from an AAS 01 aircraft (a former Heinkel He 274 bomber) and be-

The Leduc 0.21 was not capable of take-off under its own power, and had to be carried aloft and released. It could reach a top speed of Mach 0.95 (723 mph, 1,173 kph).
[© Henri Beaubois / Coll. musée de l'Air et de l'Espace - Le Bourget B 3161]

came the first aircraft to fly under ramjet power, reaching around 420 mph (680 kph) at half power. During subsequent test flights, the Leduc 0.10 reached a top speed of Mach 0.85 and a rate of climb of 7,900 feet per minute (40 m/s) to 36,000 feet (11,000 metres), thus demonstrating the potential of the ramjet as an aviation power plant.

Based on his experience with the 0.10, René Leduc built two examples of the larger Leduc 0.21 which was basically one cylinder placed into a larger one. The space between the two cylinders was the ramjet's position. Like its predecessor, the Leduc 0.21 was not capable of take-off under its own power and had to be carried aloft and released. Designed for subsonic speeds only, the 0.21 reached a top speed of Mach 0.95 (723 mph, 1,173 kph). In 1956, incorporating the experience gained from the 0.10 and 0.21 designs, the Leduc 0.22 was built as the prototype of a future Mach 2 fighter aircraft. Unlike its two predecessors, it featured swept wings and a coaxial turbojet-ramjet power plant to enable unassisted operation. While the SNECMA Atar turbojet was used for take-off, the ramjet was started during flight in order to reach high speeds. With top speed of Mach 0.97 (750 mph, 1,200 kph), the Leduc 0.22 proved unable to exceed the speed of sound due to the prohibitive drag induced by its fu-

selage shape at near-sonic speeds. The project was cancelled in favour of the more conventional Dassault Mirage III and marked the end of René Leduc's aircraft development activities.

Meanwhile, other French aircraft manufacturers also began developing high-speed aircraft, most notably Dassault Aviation near Paris, Sud-Ouest Aviation and Sud-Est-Aviation, both based in Toulouse, and Nord Aviation in Bourges. In 1950, the Nord Aviation's swept-winged Nord 1601, powered by two Rolls-Royce Derwent 5 turbojets, took to the skies to examine the aerodynamic capabilities of its prototype swept-wing design. Capable of a top speed of Mach 0.87 (621 mph, 1,080 kph), the Nord 1601 provided valuable information for subsequent high-speed designs. These included the Nord 1402 A Gerfaut which was built to intensify the studies of delta- and swept-wing designs for high-speed aircraft. The three prototypes each had slightly different wing structures and different versions of the same ATAR 101 turbojet engine. In August 1954, one Nord 1402 A Gerfaut took to the skies and broke through the sound barrier, reaching a top speed of Mach 1.28 (989 mph, 1,586 kph), thus providing more valuable information about flying at transonic and supersonic speeds.

In 1952, the French Air Force issued a specifica-

Nord Aviation built three versions of the Nord 1402A, all with different wing and engine variants.
[© Airbus]

The Dassault prototype MD.550 Mystère-Delta, predecessor to the highly successful Mirage III.
[© U.S. Navy]

tion for a supersonic fighter, with Sud-Ouest, Sud-Est, Dassault, and Nord responding. The following year, Sud-Ouest's SO 9000 Trident took to the skies as a testbed to investigate the use of two different power plants in one aircraft rather than aiming for the highest possible speed. Originally built with two Turbomeca Marbore II turbojets, one on each wingtip, and a SEPR 481 liquid rocket engine fitted in the tail, the turbojets were later replaced with two Dassault MD30 engines, a derivate of the Rolls-Royce Viper 5. With both the turbojets and the rocket engine activated, the SO 9000 Trident reached an impressive top

speed of Mach 1.63 (1,250 mph, 2,012 kph). Sud-Est's design, the SE 212 Durandal, also featured a 'hybrid' power plant consisting of a SNECMA Atar 101F turbojet and an SEPR 75 rocket engine. In December 1956, the delta-winged aircraft reached Mach 1.57 (1,200 mph, 1,940 kph). Two years later, the SE 212 Durandal's test programme was cancelled.

Dassault's design, initially known as the MD.550 Mystère-Delta and later renamed as the Mirage I, was principally powered by two Armstrong Siddeley MD30R Viper turbojets built under licence by Dassault. After reaching Mach 1.6 (1,230 mph, 1,975 kph)

The Sud-Ouest SO 9000 Trident could reach a top speed of Mach 1.63 (1,250 mph) and an altitude of 49,000 feet.
[© SNCASO / Coll. musée de l'Air et de l'Espace - Le Bourget MA 17088]

The Sud-Est SE 212 Durandal was powered by a jet engine and a rocket motor. Its top speed was Mach 1.57 (1,200 mph).
[© D.R. / Coll. musée de l'Air et de l'Espace - Le Bourget CY 8387]

in 1955, the delta-winged design evolved into the very successful Mirage III which saw service in the French Air Force as well as in numerous other countries.

In 1957, the Nord 1500 Griffon I took to the skies. The delta-winged design benefited from the experience gained from the Nord 1402 A Gerfaut and featured a dual turbo-ramjet, with the turbojet used for taking off and the ramjet producing additional thrust at speeds in excess of 600 mph (960 kph). The following year, a modified variant,

Griffon II, powered by an Atar 101E-3 turbojet and a Nord Stato-Réacteur ramjet, reached an impressive top speed of Mach 2.19 (1,680 mph, 2,700 kph). At the controls was test pilot André Turcat who would become the man to take Concorde to the skies on her maiden flight eleven years later. Although technical problems with the ramjet concept eventually led to the cancellation of the Griffon's flight tests, some of the data gained from these flights were later used in Concorde's development.

With regards to the extensive research conducted by numerous aviation manufacturers over the years in both Britain and France, the question arises as to how all this valuable data efficiently came together to eventually design, build, and test Concorde. In Britain – after a series of company takeovers and liquidations – by the late 1960s aviation was dominated by the British Aircraft Corporation (BAC) and Hawker Siddeley. When the Anglo-French treaty to build Concorde was signed in 1962, BAC,

with all the British research under its belt, was the main player on Britain's side of the project.

In France, the research and testing conducted by various aviation companies, also furthered the French experience in the design of supersonic technology. In 1957, the two state-owned aviation manufacturers Sud-Ouest and Sud-Est, belonging to the various companies which had made significant contributions to the French knowledge of supersonic technology, came together to form Sud Aviation,

Test pilot André Turcat (fifth from right with sunglasses) and his team posing in front of the Nord 1500 Griffon II in 1957.
[© Vazken / CC BY-SA 4.0]

BAC's future Concorde partner. It might be surprising that Dassault Aviation, a leader in supersonic technology and the manufacturer of the Mirage III - Western Europe's first military jet to exceed Mach 2 in horizontal flight - did not participate in the development of Concorde. During negotiations as to who was going to get what share in the Concorde programme, it can be speculated that Dassault was more interested in leading the project than being a contributor. With this being impossible, Dassault decided not to participate.

The design of the deltawinged Dassault Mirage III was influenced in part by the British Fairey Delta 2. The successful Mirage was sold to numerous other countries, including Australia, as seen in this photo taken in 1980.
[© U.S. Air Force]

The Anglo-French Partnership

With Europe slowly recovering from the horrors of World War II and Britain's pilots making the first supersonic test flights in 1948, the British de Havilland company was not only working on military jet designs, but also on a civilian jet-powered aircraft. Named the DH. 106 Comet, it was designed as a pressurized passenger aircraft, with thirty-six seats, capable of flying across the Atlantic. With a cruising speed of 450 mph (725 kph), flights on the Comet were about twice as fast as on advanced piston-engined aircraft of the day such as the Douglas DC-6. Her four Halford H.2 Ghost (later replaced with four Rolls-Royce Avon) turbojets ran smoothly and were less noisy than piston engines and had low maintenance costs. Moreover, they enabled the airliner to fly above weather which other aircraft had to fly through. Despite the advances with delta-wing designs gained from military test aircraft, the Comet's designers decided to build her with swept wings and a conventional tail.

After her maiden flight on 27 July 1949 as the world's first jet airliner, planned for production, flight test observer Tony Fairbrother commented: "The Comet must have been one of the all-time technical achievements. I don't think it is too much to say that the world changed from the moment its wheels left the ground." (*Aeroplane Monthly*, August 1989). The British minister of supply, Duncan Sandys, went even further by describing the Comet as an integral part of the nation's economic future: "During the next few years, the UK has an opportunity, which may not recur, of developing aircraft manufacture as one of our main export industries. On whether we grasp this opportunity and so establish firmly an industry of the utmost strategic and economic importance, our future as a great nation may depend." (H. Trischler & S. Zeilinger, *Tackling Transport*, Vol. 3, 2003).

The de Havilland DH. 106 Comet was the world's jet-powered commercial airliner.
[© British Airways]

The Sud Aviation SE 210 Caravelle, powered by two Rolls-Royce Avon turbojets, was a very successful European first-generation jetliner.
[© Air France Museum]

The first airline to order this innovative aircraft was the British Overseas Airways Corporation (BOAC), the forerunner to British Airways. After her introduction to commercial service in 1952, numerous international airlines, including Air France, ordered and operated the Comet. However, within a year of entering service, problems began to emerge, with three aircraft lost after suffering catastrophic in-flight break-ups. The Comet was withdrawn from service and extensively tested. The investigation identified various design and construction flaws, including improper riveting and dangerous concentrations of stress around the rectangular-shaped windows and openings in the fuselage. As a result, the Comet was extensively redesigned, with various structural reinforcements and oval windows – the latter becoming standard in aircraft to this day. Although sales never fully recovered, subsequent further developments of the Comet eventually culminated in the Comet 4 in 1958 which had a productive career of more than thirty years.

Competing aircraft manufacturers heeded the lessons learned from the Comet and implemented them in their own designs, the Boeing 707, Douglas DC-8, Convair 880, and the French Sud Aviation SE 210 Caravelle. The latter, which began its successful commercial service in 1959, was the world's first jet-powered airliner developed for the short/medium-range market.

Based on the design work and operational experience gained from the Comet and the Caravelle, aircraft designers and engineers on both sides of the English Channel began making plans for the next generation of jet-powered commercial airliners.

The late 1950s and early 1960s saw the spectacular beginnings of the American-Soviet space race – the ultimate technological challenge for designers, engineers, and pilots (newly known as astronauts or cosmonauts) alike. Inspired by the early achievements in space exploration and with military jet fighters and bombers capable of flying at supersonic speeds, it seemed natural that even fare-paying civilian travellers would soon fly to international destinations faster than the speed of sound.

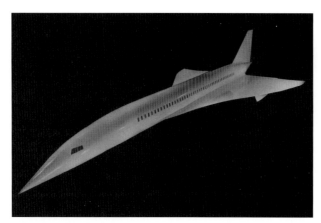

Model of the projected Super Caravelle. She and the British Bristol 223 formed the basis for Concorde.
[© Air France Museum]

'Entente Concordiale'

In Britain, under the leadership of Sir Morien Morgan, the Supersonic Transport Aircraft Committee (STAC) based in Farnborough began to investigate the creation of a civilian supersonic airliner in 1956. As a result, funded by the STAC, various British aviation firms developed different designs. By 1960, after the forced merger of most of these firms, the Bristol 223 design was selected as the basis for a British supersonic airliner capable of carrying about a hundred passengers across the Atlantic at a speed around Mach 2. At the same time, the French state-owned aviation firm Sud Aviation was developing the design of the smaller but similar-shaped Super Caravelle as a supersonic successor to the Caravelle, capable of up to Mach 2 and able to carry seventy passengers on routes within Europe

and to destinations in Africa across the Mediterranean.

With the British and the French concepts on the drawing boards, the governments of both nations became aware that the design and manufacture of a supersonic airliner would require an overseas partner to share the enormous costs. At the same time the Americans were beginning to work on their own supersonic airliner called SST (Supersonic Transport). Although the British initially intended to establish a cooperation agreement with the United States, this did not happen as American aviation firms were focusing on designs capable of speeds up to Mach 3 while the British were concentrating on Mach 2.

Finally, the governments of Britain and France came together and negotiated the formation of a consortium to share the develop-

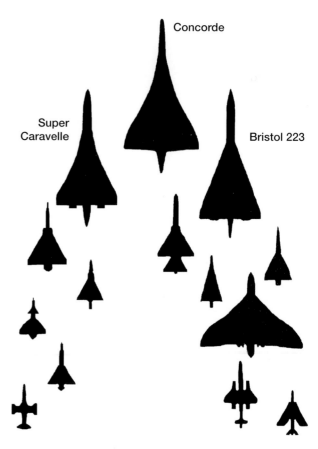

Concorde's family tree. Derived from early military aircraft, the Bristol 223 and Super Caravelle were the analogous, direct antecedents of Concorde.

ment and production costs for a supersonic airliner on a 50/50 split based on the Bristol 223 and the Super Caravelle. On 29 November 1962, the agreement was jointly signed by the British minister for aviation, Julian Amery, and the French ambassador, Geoffrey de Courcel, thus giving birth to the Anglo-French Concorde project. Although the French, under the leadership of Robert Vergnaud, the director of civil air transport, had wanted two airliners to be built as a result of the cooperation: a larger, long-

range aircraft based on the Type 223 and a medium-range version similar to their Super Caravelle. After receiving feedback from potential buyers it became clear that there was only interest in a long-range supersonic airliner, leading to the cancellation of the smaller variant in order to concentrate all available resources on a transatlantic aircraft. Both partners agreed to build two prototypes – one named '001' to be constructed in Toulouse in France, and '002' to be built simultaneously in Filton in Britain.

Based on the experience with the powerful and proven Bristol Olympus turbojet which had been the power plant for the Royal Air Force's Avro Vulcan bomber for several years, it was decided to further develop this engine to power Concorde.

Development and Construction

When the treaty to build Concorde was signed, supersonic flight was already a reality – at least for a few elite pilots in a handful of air forces around the world. What was new was the idea to fly one hundred fare-paying passengers from London and Paris across the Atlantic and to other overseas destinations in comfort and without flight suits or oxygen masks. In order to achieve this Herculean task, the British Aircraft Corporation (BAC) and Sud Aviation (Aérospatiale as of 1970), the two firms driving the project, worked closely with more than 800 different British and French subcontractors employing the brightest designers, engineers, aerodynamicists, scientists, technicians and factory workers. This enormous number of companies, whose work had to be coordinated in order to deliver their completed parts to the main manufacturers in Toulouse and Filton, resulted in a complexity never before seen in civil aviation history, thus requiring close cooperation between the French and British teams working as they were in two different countries. Therefore, many members of the Concorde project had to overcome the language barrier and learn either French or English to establish a solid means of communication and information exchange.

In order to honour the 50/50 split defined by the treaty signed in 1962, bureaucrats in both nations often chose the subcontractors on political rather than practical (or time- and cost-efficient) grounds. As a result, there were numerous examples in which a company in either Britain or France received a contract to design or construct a particular device for Concorde although a company in the respective other country might be better suited for the task. These impractical decisions, in combination with the immense complexity of the programme, caused various delays in the completion of the two prototypes.

Sections of Concorde's structure were 'sculpted' out of big pieces of solid aluminium (AU2GN), making them very strong.
[© BAE Systems]

A	FUSELAGE NOSE	B.A.C. WEYBRIDGE
B	DROOP NOSE	B.A.C. HURN
C	FORWARD FUSELAGE	B.A.C. WEYBRIDGE
D	REAR FUSELAGE	B.A.C. WEYBRIDGE
E	FIN	B.A.C. WEYBRIDGE
F	RUDDER	B.A.C. WEYBRIDGE
NACELLES COMPRISING:		
G	AIR INTAKE	B.A.C. PRESTON
H	ENGINE BAY	B.A.C. FILTON
J	NOZZLES	SNECMA
K	ENGINES	ROLLS ROYCE — BRISTOL
L	INTERMEDIATE FUSELAGE	MARIGNANE
M	CENTRE WING (41 - 46)	MARIGNANE
N	FORWARD WING	NANTES
P	CENTRE WING (46 - 54)	NANTES
Q	CENTRE WING (54 - 60)	TOULOUSE
R	CENTRE WING (60 - 66)	TOULOUSE
S	ELEVONS	BOUGUENAIS
T	CENTRE WING (66 - 72)	ST. NAZAIRE
U	OUTER WING	BOURGES
V	LANDING GEAR MAIN	HISPANO SUIZA
V_1	MAIN WHEELS & BRAKES	DUNLOP
W	LANDING GEAR NOSE	MESSIER
X	WING FAIRING FWD	B.A.C. FILTON
X_1	WING FAIRING AFT	B.A.C. WEYBRIDGE
Y	DORSAL FIN	B.A.C. FILTON
Z	RADOME	B.A.C. STEVENAGE

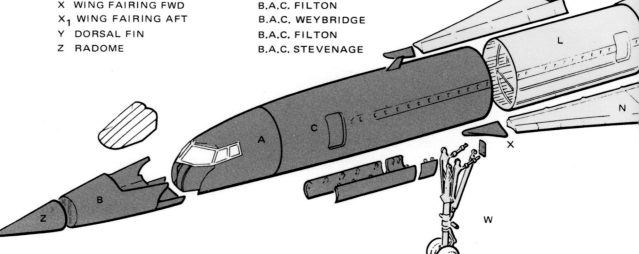

The building process for the total number of twenty Concordes basically followed the same pattern but evolved between the first two prototypes, the two pre-production aircraft and the sixteen later production ones as prototype testing resulted in some design modifications requiring different manufacturing techniques. These alterations ranged from minor changes to elaborate revisions. The most significant difference between the two prototypes and the later variants were the nose and visor, the wings and the rear section of the fuselage.

First the central fuselage was assembled, with the wings pre-attached, from the six sections built in various locations in France. Then the British-manufactured nose and tail sections were added, followed by the completion of the wings, the addition of further external parts such as the rudder, and the fitting of the landing gear. Next came the fitting of the four Olympus 593 engines. After the installation

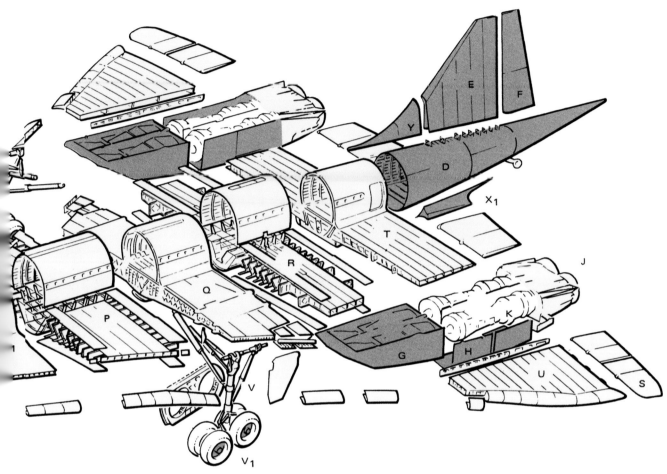

As determined in the 1962 treaty, the work to design and build Concorde was shared on an equal basis between France and Britain as shown in this illustration. All the French and British components were assembled at two locations: Toulouse where the French Concordes were built, and Filton where the British sisters were produced.
[© BAE Systems]

of miles of wiring throughout Concorde's interior, the airframe finally received its numerous instruments and technical equipment on the flight deck (cockpit), and the cabin fixtures such as panelling, seats, carpets, toilets and galleys.

Philip Cairns who later would become a licensed ground engineer for Concorde helped build the British prototype 002 (G-SST):

"I was always impressed by the amount of care and inspections that were carried out as the construction progressed. This gave the whole Concorde project a certain integrity and with this as a background I was always aware that Concorde was truly a quality aircraft. This helped me to be focused on maintaining this aircraft to the best of my ability. It was a privilege to be on the Concorde fleet to the very end. My philosophy was if I look after Concorde well, she would look after me. I loved my job and looking back now I would do it all again, I had a most satisfying and fulfilling career."

Air hostesses under the wooden mock-up. Concorde's potential customers – the world's leading airlines – are represented among the hostesses' uniforms: TWA, Air France, BOAC, Lufthansa, Japan Air Lines, Air India, Braniff.
[© BAE Systems]

A model of Concorde during the extensive wind tunnel tests.
[© BAE Systems]

Mock-up of Concorde's flight deck. The layout of the pilots' instruments was (and still is) critical to flight safety.
[© Air France Museum]

HRH Prince Philip visits the mock-up of Concorde's flight deck in Toulouse, 1965. During one of the first flights of the British prototype 002, he would take the controls. Philip later became a friend of Brian Trubshaw, Britain's chief Concorde test pilot.
[© Toulouse City Archives, André Cros Coll.,CC BY-SA 4.0]

Prototype 001 during construction in Toulouse. The fuselage and the wings have not been painted yet.
[© Rolls-Royce]

Prototype 001 nearing completion, 1967. Visitors were allowed to have a look at the aircraft.
[All images except where noted: © Toulouse City Archives, André Cros Coll., CC BY-SA 4.0]

Transport of a completed fuselage section for final assembly in Toulouse.

The transportation of the various sections of Concorde to their final assembly sites in Toulouse or Filton took place by rail, lorry or aircraft.

Prototype 001 during an 'open door' event for the general public in Toulouse, 1968.

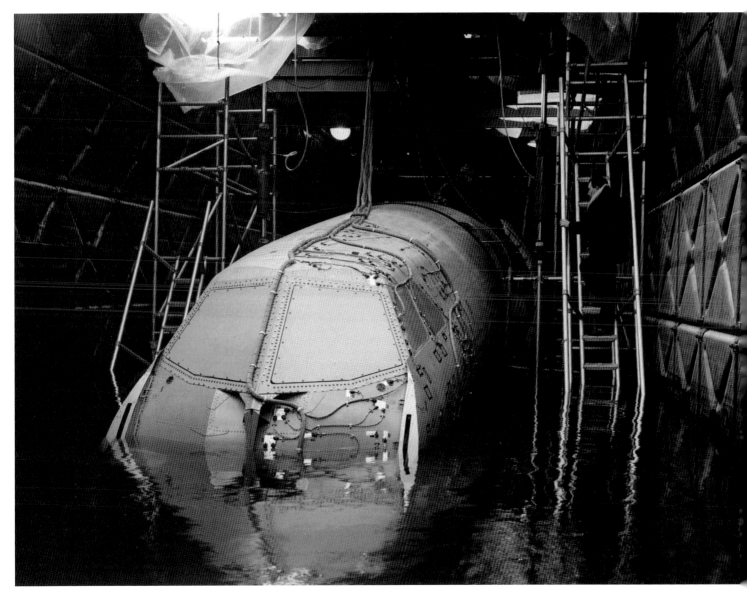

Testing Concorde's fuselage pressure in the water tank, probably at Filton.
[© BAE Systems]

Opposite: Pre-production Concorde 102's droop nose and visor (made in Filton) being checked in Toulouse. During construction of the prototpyes (001 and 002), the glass required for the fully glazed visor capable of supersonic flight was still under development. Therefore, the proto-types had to be fitted with small cut-out sections allowing the pilots a limited forward visibility. The two pre-produc-tion aircraft 101 and 102 were the first to be built with fully glazed visors, thus giving the pilots a much better forward visibility.
[© BAE Systems]

Watch Video:

Develop-
ment &
Cons-
truction

Please see instructions
on page 2.

An Avro Vulcan as a flying testbed for the Olympus 593 engine (centre) which is shown here during ice trials. These tests showed how far the build-up of ice within the intake and the first compression stages could affect the engine's performance. This image shows how much bigger Concorde's Olympus engines were compared to the ones used for the Vulcan.
[© Rolls-Royce]

Assembling a pair of the Rolls-Royce/SNECMA Olympus turbojets. During Concorde's development the Olympus engine evolved from the original 593 model to the 593-610-14-28, the final version fitted to the production aircraft.
[© Rolls-Royce]

Completion of a fuselage section. Its maximum external width is 9 feet 5 inches (2.87m), the maximum height 10 feet 10 inches (3.3m).
[© Air France Museum]

Artistic depiction for Concorde's lavatory by
Charles Butler and Associates.
[© British Airways]

Concept for a first-class cabin layout which was never
used: Concorde only had one class.
[© British Airways]

Pre-production Concorde 101 under assembly, 1969. The
French-made wings were shipped to Filton in Britain.
[© BAE Systems]

Concorde's Roll-Out

Five years after the signing of the Anglo-French treaty to build the world's first commercial supersonic airliner, the day had finally come to officially present Concorde to the public. The officially ceremony took place in Toulouse on 11 December 1967, with more than 1,100 guests present. This first public appearance was intended – through TV, newspapers and magazines – to give the world, and in particular the French and British taxpayers, a chance to see 'their' Concorde 'in the flesh'. It was a very cold and clear winter day. A French military band played before the official ceremony began. Then the hangar doors started to open to reveal the absolutely unbelievably beautiful shape of Concorde prototype 001 ('Zero-zero-un') which had been assembled in Toulouse.

Then the British Minister of Technology, Tony Benn, and the French Minister of Transportation, Jean Chamant, entered the hangar and cut the tapes across the hangar doors. Representatives from the option-holding airlines were present along with their respective cabin crew members who posed for photographs in front of the aircraft. Flight attendant Marne Davis wore a futuristic-looking astronaut's helmet to match the aircraft that had just been unveiled. Then the taxi-tug driver came out and pulled on a special pair of white gloves, climbed up into his vehicle and slowly moved Concorde out of the hangar with the nose right over the heads of the

Roll-out ceremony of prototype 001 at Toulouse on 11 December 1967. The British Minister of Technology, Tony Benn, is at right.
[All images except where noted: © Toulouse City Archives, André Cros Coll., CC BY-SA 4.0]

Concorde 001 inside her hangar before being revealed to the public. Note the logos of the airliners which had placed their orders for Concorde.

A flight attendant poses in a flight suit-like uniform to demonstrate Concorde's futuristic design.

Tony Benn (centre) and Jean Chamant (right) are ready to cut the tape, thus 'allowing' Concorde to be rolled out.
[All images: © Toulouse City Archives, André Cros Coll., CC BY-SA 4.0]

Tony Benn greets airline pilots and flight attendants posing in front of Concorde.
[© British Airways]

A French military band providing the musical accompaniment during the roll-out ceremony.

heads. The French test pilot, André Turcat, and Brian Trubshaw, his British counterpart, attended the ceremony. At that point there was no doubt that any pilot would want to fly Concorde. Nearly a year later, on 19 September 1968, the British prototype, Concorde 002, was unveiled to the public at the British Aircraft Corporation's manufacturing plant at Filton in Bristol.

To build these two first Concordes was a great achievement and the work of tens of thousands of dedicated scientists, engineers, designers, and factory workers. But there was still much work to be done and months of painstaking checks and ground testing lay ahead before both aircraft were ready to make their maiden flights.

Watch Video: Concorde Roll-Out

Please see instructions on page 2.

The French Concorde chief test pilot, André Turcat (centre), and his British counterpart, Brian Trubshaw (left) witness Concorde's roll-out.

The Maiden Flights

*"As you can see, she flies and,
in addition, I can say she flies well."*

– André Turcat, pilot of Concorde prototype 001

Concorde Prototype 001

On 2 March 1969, a clear and crisp spring day, Concorde prototype 001 (registration F-WTSS) made her maiden flight. With the project going back to 1962, for everyone involved this was an emotional day. Numerous guests from the aviation business and hundreds of journalists from all over the world had arrived to witness the flight; TV crews were ready to broadcast the flight to every continent. The flight was to have taken place the previous day, but heavy mist forced the chief pilot André Turcat to postpone it until 2 March. Loudspeakers informed the waiting crowd that Concorde 001 was ready. After firing up her four mighty engines, one after another, the elegant craft moved down the perimeter track and turned slowly to line up on the runway. Meanwhile, trucks equipped with noisy klaxons drove up and down the tarmac to chase any birds away, a serious threat if hitting the engines during take-off. After releasing the brakes, Concorde 001 began to move down the runway carrying the hopes and dreams of thousands of people who had contributed to the most ambitious technological project in European history. After gathering speed, she lifted her nose and climbed into the sky. This moment marked the beginning of a love affair that would last for nearly three decades. Everyone who witnessed the flight was deeply touched. After about twenty-seven minutes, Concorde 001 came into view again, made her approach. As the wheels touched the runway, she deployed the tail parachute and engaged reverse thrust to slow down. Concorde's maiden flight made a powerful impression on the crew. After a safe landing, the crew was applauded and cheered by the crowd. Frank Debouck, who later would become the Concorde manager for Air France, watched on television this significant event in aviation history:

"It was a moment of great emotion and pride. And a few months later, the first steps on the moon were taken. What struck me most was André Turcat's comment after the aircraft had landed: 'As you can see, she flies and, in addition, I can say she flies well.' It was definitely great events like this that motivated me to consider a career as an engineer. But at that time, I did not imagine that I one day would be commercially responsible for supersonic flight."

Pierre Grange who would become an Air France Concorde co-pilot in the 1980s, also remembers the maiden flight:

"Like all French, I was in front of a TV to view the first flight of 001 in Toulouse. I was then in pilot training and the room was buzzing with enthusiasm. As for 002, we weren't too interested. All the significant first flights – maiden flight, Mach 1 and Mach 2 flights – were flown with 001, and we had the impression that everything was happening at home."

Across the English Channel, John Hutchinson, a pilot in the Royal Air Force who would become a British Concorde captain in the 1970s, was also impressed: "I certainly watched the maiden flight out of Toulouse and I think Raymond Baxter's commentary ['She flies, she flies.'] still makes all the hairs on the back of my neck stand on end. It was a brilliant piece of commentating by him."

Watch Video:
Maiden Flight

Please see instructions on page 2.

Before Concorde 001 could take to the skies, she had to pass numerous tests on the ground, including various taxiing trials.
[© Airbus]

Concorde 001 as seen through one of the two openings of the engine test bay at Toulouse.
[© Airbus]

Frenchwoman Jacqueline Auriol (1917–2000) attends Concorde's maiden flight. During her exceptional flying career she broke the women's air speed record several times. Later, Auriol became the first woman to fly Concorde, only to be succeeded by two more, Barbara Harmer and Béatrice Vialle.
(All images except where noted: © Toulouse City Archives, André Cros Coll., CC BY-SA 4.0)

The crew on Concorde's maiden flight, from left: Michel Retif (flight test engineer in the cockpit), André Turcat (captain), Henri Perrier (flight test engineer in the cabin with the test equipment) and Jacques Guignard (flight test pilot in the right seat next to Captain Turcat).
[© Bernard Pourchet]

Concorde 001 during the moment of her very first take-off. British TV commentator Raymond Baxter excitedly shouted: "… her nose comes up to thirty degrees …"

"… she is airborne … she flies …" With these words André Turcat took Concorde to the skies for her first flight which lasted just twenty-seven minutes.
[© Airbus]

Concorde lands safely, deploying the tail parachute and engaging reverse thrust to slow down.
[© B. Pourchet]

André Turcat and his crew disembark Concorde 001 after their historic maiden flight to receive congratulations from the ground crew.
[Both images: © Toulouse City Archives, André Cros Coll.,CC BY-SA 4.0]

During the subsequent press conference, a very pleased André Turcat enthuses about Concorde's great performance on her maiden flight.

Concorde Prototype 002

Just weeks after Concorde 001 had taken to the skies, her sister 002 (G-BSST) followed suit on 9 April 1969. The event took place at the airfield at Filton, Bristol, where the same crowd of spectators and journalists gathered to witness the maiden flight of the second prototype. The crew for that flight was chief pilot Brian Trubshaw, co-pilot John Cochrane, and engineer Brian Watts. Before the successful flight two high-speed taxi runs with a speed up to 120 knots had been aborted due a failure flag on the captain's airspeed indicator. As 002 had been cleared for flight before each of the two previous taxi runs, Turbshaw decided that – if his instruments worked reliably – on the third run he would take off with Concorde 002 for the first time. Nigel Ferris who had helped to build 002 was there on that memorable day:

"The crew went on board, began their pre-flight checks, started the engines and moved out to the end of the runway facing west. Then she began to roll, the back boilers [reheats] kicked in, and halfway down reached V1 [speed], rotated and lifted into the air. 'Smokey Joe' was airborne, a tremendous sight and sound, and the beginning of an adventure which has seen me follow the aircraft ever since, in the absolute knowledge that I had seen her built and had some insight into how it was done. A true privilege, with awe and wonder that such a beautiful and advanced aircraft should show off, I felt, just for me."

Twenty-two minutes after taking off from Filton Trubshaw made his approach at the RAF station at Fairford, fifty miles to the north-east as the Filton runway was too short for the requirements of the subsequent test flights. Therefore, RAF Fairford had been equipped as the main Concorde flight test centre. Despite the failure of both radar altimeters, and the crew being thirty-five feet above the landing gear, Trubshaw landed flawlessly. After disembarking, the crew was greeted by a cheering crowd. Both André Turcat and Brian Trubshaw had made aviation history.

A French postcard commemorating Concorde's maiden flight on 2 March 1969.
[© Bernard Pourchet]

Thousands of spectators welcome Concorde 002
as she arrives at Fairford on her maiden flight.
[© British Airways]

The British prototype, Concorde 002, also known as 'Smokey Joe', takes to the skies at Filton for the first time on 9 April 1969.
[© Airbus]

Concorde 002 lands at Fairford after twenty-two minutes.
[© Airbus]

Supersonic Pioneers

André Turcat

On 2 March 1969, André Turcat (1921–2016) became the first person ever to fly Concorde. A test pilot of international standing, he joined Sud Aviation in the early 1960s and was made the director of flight testing and Concorde's chief test pilot. More than just an aviator, Turcat later went on to become deputy mayor of Toulouse and a member of the European Parliament.
[© Toulouse City Archives, CC BY-SA 4.0]

Brian Trubshaw

On 9 April 1969, Brian Trubshaw (1924–2001) became the first pilot to fly the British Concorde prototype 002. The director and general manager of flight operations of the Filton divison of BAC, Trubshaw was responsible for the British Concorde's flight tests. Like Turcat, he was an experienced and respected test pilot and had been Vickers' chief test pilot before joining BAC. He gained a deserved reputation for absolute calm under pressure when he safely landed the Vickers VC-10 prototype after he'd lost control of an elevator that was flapping violently due to the failure of a hinge bracket.
[© Toulouse City Archives, CC BY-SA 4.0]

Testing

Over the next few years, Concorde was subjected to the most extensive test programme of any aircraft in the history of civil aviation. When she received her certification of airworthiness in December 1975 she had flown more than 5,500 hours including 2,000 hours at supersonic speed. This intense programme of endurance flying was completed in September 1975, after 750 hours in the air.

The ground test programme included the construction of two complete airframes which were installed in full-scale test-rigs. The first one was built at the French establishment in Toulouse for static tests; the second at the Royal Aircraft Establishment in Farnborough, Hampshire, to examine the effects of flight operations on the aircraft's structure over a long period of time. Various fatigue tests exposed Concorde to combinations of severe stress and extreme temperatures. Before certification, more than 20,000 simulated flying hours had been completed. In order to test the numerous aircraft systems and components, various additional rigs were built. In September 1975, Concorde's engine, the Olympus 593, received its certificate for supersonic passenger service. With more than 54,000 hours of engine testing, its test programme became the most extensive for a civilian aircraft: 22,000 hours took place in flight with 8,000 hours at supersonic speeds, and the remainder in ground test beds. The tests demonstrated the engine's ability to be started at extremely cold and hot temperatures and to withstand the impact of dust, hailstones, and even birds.

Concorde in front of the engine test bay in Toulouse during a performance test of her Olympus engines.
[All images: © Toulouse City Archives, André Cros Coll., CC BY-SA 4.0]

Concorde in front of the engine run detuner to reduce noise and exhaust fumes.

Concorde prototypes 001 (right) and 002 (left) together in 1971. Although identical, prototype 001 (F-WTSS) can be distinguished from her twin sister 002 (G-BSST) by the different paint scheme on her vertical stabilizer.

Flight test engineer Henri Perrier in the French prototype's cabin with the test equipment. During the early test flights the crew had to wear pressure suits, oxygen masks and parachutes. For emergency bailouts the prototypes and preproduction aircraft featured downward escape hatches. Bailing out at Mach 2 at 60,000 feet, however, leaves any chance of survival at slim to zero.
[All images: © Airbus]

Watch Video:

Testing

Please see instructions on page 2.

The French pre-production aircraft Sierra Alpha (F-WTSA) at Fairbanks, Alaska, for cold temperature trials, 1974. She was the first aircraft to have the final production shape and dimensions of Concorde.

Sierra Alpha (F-WTSA) was used for the development of new engines, and in a considerable number of rolling runway tests for, amongst other things, the certification of the new carbon brakes, the water deflectors and thrust reversers. When Sierra Alpha attended the opening of the Dallas-Fort Worth Airport in 1973 she became the first Concorde to visit the United States.

On later test flights crew members dispensed with pressure suits, oxygen masks and parachutes as they had developed a certain trust in their aircraft.

THE DESIGN OF A MARVEL

*"The first time I saw Concorde gave me the feeling
that I was boarding a 'racing beast'."*

– Patrick Sevestre, former AF ground engineer

*"Concorde has an aesthetic that, although born from
the necessities of supersonic flight aerodynamics,
is a true work of art."*

– Philippe Gebarowski, Concorde passenger

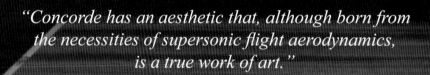

Concorde's distinctive and beautiful shape is the result of the masterful work of her engineers and extensive wind tunnel testing.
[© Spencer Wilmot]

In order to design an aircraft that could fly hundred passengers comfortably at speeds previously only achieved by military fighters, the Anglo-French teams had to overcome numerous technical challenges. To create the best aerodynamic shape and a powerplant capable to achieve the desired speed operating in the extreme conditions of supersonic flight, extensive research and development work was necessary. This work and the subsequent production were spread across Britain and France. It was the combination of the expertise of Sud Aviation France, the British Aircraft Corporation, Bristol Siddeley Engines (Rolls-Royce) and Snecma which succeeded to produce the formidable Concorde design. Eventually, two final assembly lines were built, one in Filton and one in Toulouse. Ian Kirby who worked as a flight engineer for twenty-two years on Concorde for British Airways, summarizes her unique capabilities by recalling on of his flights:

"Concorde was the meeting of theory and practice to produce a machine that was beautiful to look at and did its unique job where all others failed. That is charisma. Concorde used reheat to increase thrust for the acceleration from Mach 0.95 to Mach 1.7. At Mach 1.7 the reheats were selected off and Concorde was the only aircraft that could continue to accelerate and climb to Mach 2 at 50,000 feet and then continue to climb at Mach 2. On one flight, a U. S. Marine pilot sat next to me in the jump seat. When I told him I was about to turn off the reheats he asked if we were going to slow down. Concorde showed him that was not the case. He remarked that had he cancelled reheat at Mach 1.7 in his Phantom F-4 it would have felt like he had hit a brick wall. No other aircraft could do what Concorde did and the biggest breakthrough was the design of the intake system that, in the cruise, produced over 50 per cent of the total thrust."

▶ Watch Video:

Flying Concorde

Please see instructions on page 2.

The Ogee Delta Wing

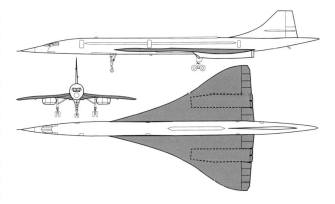

Because of Concorde's incredibly top speed of Mach 2 (1,350 mph), her fuselage and wings were designed to a very different shape compared to traditional airliners. Numerous individual shapes had to be tested using various wind tunnel models before the designers made the decision in favour of the 'ogee delta' wing which gave Concorde her iconic shape. To minimize friction, the airframe had to be narrower and far more tapered at the front and back than subsonic airliners.

The almost triangular 'ogee delta' wing, with its S-curved leading edge, gave acceptable lift and drag at all speeds, including take-off and landing, and provided a large internal volume for the fuel. The shape with its clever curves produced the lift required at all speeds. Former Air France Concorde pilot Gérard Duval explains: "When we reduced speed during the approach before landing we had to increase the pitch i.e. the angle of attack to maintain the lift. As the angle of attack increased the vortexes appeared, got stronger and created additional lift."

While flying at supersonic speeds, Concorde's wing design was long, sleek and narrow enough to prevent excessive drag. Concorde did not use separate ailerons and elevators but combined them in the form of six 'elevons' (a word that combines elevator and aileron) that worked together to control the pitch and roll of the aircraft. Fuel tanks were located throughout the wings and fuselage. To keep the aircraft levelled at high speeds, the fuel management system adjusted the weight distribution by

Concorde's 'ogee delta' wing, with its S-curved leading edge. Ogive curves and surfaces are used in engineering, architecture and woodworking.
[© Air France Museum]

Concorde did not use separate ailerons and elevators but combined them in the form of six 'elevons' to control the aircraft's pitch and roll.
[© British Airways]

pumping fuel between different tanks to move the centre of gravity forward or back.

Ian Kirby is still impressed by the wings' formidable design: "The flight characteristics were like few other aircraft. On the approach it was on the back side of the drag curve, meaning that as you flew slower the drag increased. It was also very responsive in roll but had far more inertia in pitch."

Concorde's delta wing ran for most of the fuselage's length. It was capable of good aerodynamic performance at low and high speeds.
[Top: © Bob Ware / bottom: © Vicentiu Ciorlaus]

The Engines and Air Intakes

Concorde was designed with four Olympus 593 engines, mounted in pairs. Each of these was capable of producing 32,000-pound thrust, and with the use of reheat each could reach 38,000-pound thrust. Philip Cairns, a former licensed ground engineer for twenty-seven years at British Airways, explains:

"Besides the Soviet Tupolev Tu-144, Concorde was the first airliner to have reheat; this extra power was used on take-off and again to send the aircraft through the sound barrier and onwards up to Mach 1.7 from where Concorde would continue to accelerate up to Mach 2.02. The engine however was one of three components in the propulsion unit, the others being the intakes and the primary and secondary nozzle. The intakes provided 25 per cent of

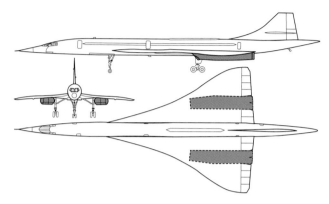

thrust as did the primary and secondary nozzles. The engine itself was a twin spool engine; the low-pressure shaft ran through the high-pressure shaft. The engine was extremely well designed and very tough. The environment it lived in was quite hostile, as it continued to work very hard through the whole flight. The intakes were responsible for this as they still produced quite a relative high pressure at the engine face compared to other commercial aircraft engines. The four engines were closely monitored during flight by the flight engineer and the intakes played an important role in the flight of Concorde as turbine engines can only ever accept air at 0.5 Mach (half the speed of sound)."

For Concorde's four engines to work best, the air

needed to enter them at a subsonic speed of around 350 mph. But given the aircraft's top speed of 1,350 mph, the air would have entered the engines too fast for them to work efficiently. In order to control the speed of the incoming air, each of the four engines was fitted with a specially designed air-intake system – a complex series of ramps that automatically moved to just the right position to keep the air travelling into the engine at 350 mph independently from Concorde's speed. The movements of these ramps were controlled by a digital computer system adjusting them constantly in order to adapt them to changes in speed and conditions. The intakes produced just over half the thrust of the powerplant when cruising at Mach 2 to

Each Olympus engine was capable of producing 32,000-pound thrust, and with the use of reheat each could reach 38,000-pound thrust.
[© Rolls-Royce]

Concorde's wing shape and the position of her Olympus engines and air intakes.
[© Art Brett]

2.04. The engines ran faster in the cruise than they did on take-off. *Gérard Duval points out:* "Concorde's air-intake system was a revolutionary design and a closely guarded secret due to *its very high efficiency.*"

Concorde's air-intake system not only controlled the speed of the air entering her engines but also generated some of the thrust to reach and maintain its incredible top speed.
[© Gérard Duval]

Left: The prototype Concorde 001: close-up of engines, with the scalloped thrust reversers prominent.
Right: Production aircraft F-BTSD with the revised design of 'eyelid' variable nozzle/thrust reverser.

Concorde's four powerful reheats light up as she climbs after her take-off. Each produced an extra 6,000-pound thrust.
[© Johnathan Safford]

The Fuel System

Concorde's fuel system was huge and complex, thus fulfilling various tasks as Philip Cairns explains:

"Concorde's fuel system is huge, there are thirteen fuel tanks numbered 1 to 11. The reason for this is that tanks 5 and 7 each have an extra tank numbered 5a and 7a, these tanks would then feed their parent tanks only. The tanks were arranged in a way that would help the aircraft's trim and also in a way that would move the centre of gravity rearwards and forward again. In supersonic cruise the fuel would be towards the rear, helping to trim the aircraft so it would always look to be climbing, which in fact it was. Coming back into land the fuel would be moved forwards. This was done by an automatic system and was set up before flight, and was monitored throughout the flight by the flight engineer. Tanks 1, 2, 3 and 4 fed their respective engines, i.e. No. 1 engine would be fed by tank No. 1 and so on. You could cross-feed to the other engines as well. Fuel was used for cooling the aircraft, the hydraulic oil, the cooling air, and also used in the heat exchangers for various tasks … Refuelling Concorde was an art form and most engineers enjoyed doing it. A full fuel load on Concorde could be 96,000 kilograms or 96 tonnes. Most fuel loads to cross the Atlantic were usually over 90 tonnes with a lighter load coming back due to prevailing winds."

Right: After the tragic crash of Sierra Charlie (F-BTSC) in 2000, the Concorde fleet was fitted with Kevlar liners inside their tanks to reinforce their robustness.

Bottom: Concorde required engineers slender enough to squeeze inside the fuel tanks for maintenance and repair work.
[both: © British Airways]

The Droop Nose

"It was a necessary piece of aircraft design for Concorde, so the pilot could see where he was going when landing and taxiing around the airfield."

– Philip Cairns, Concorde ground engineer

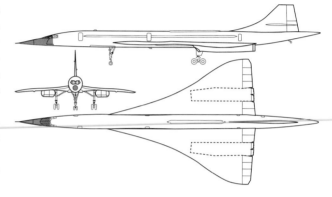

An integral part of Concorde was her celebrated 'droop nose' appearance. The aircraft needed a long, thin and streamlined nose to cut through the air in front of it in order to reduce drag when flying at supersonic speeds. During take-off and landing, Concorde needed to fly at a very steep angle in relation to the ground, thus ensuring that the wing could generate enough lift at the low speeds required. In order to enable the two pilots in the cockpit to see the runway in front of them during take-off and landing, Concorde's nose could be lowered, or 'drooped' down. Inserted by the bayonet fitting into the nose was the reserve pitot which measured Con-

corde's speed through the air. The principal tubes were located on the under-side of the aircraft's fuse-lage. Philip Cairns explains the various positions of the droop nose:

"This was new feature for an airliner to have, but it was so essential for Concorde because the way she landed her nose would be pointing up, so to get a good view of the runway the nose would be lowered fully down to 12.5°; when taxiing the nose would be raised to 5°, and finally when she was on the stand the nose was brought up 0° and the retractable visor would be put back to fully up. The droop nose was fully up in 'super cruise' [supersonic flight] along

with the retractable visor. Another feature which was good for the crew was when the aircraft took off and all the landing gear was retracted; the last piece of the nose to go up was the visor, and when this happened the flight deck became very quiet as all the wind noise was cut out."

Former Air France Concorde pilot Pierre Grange remembers: "[During the approach] the nose – and with it the visor – was lowered as late as possible as it produced additional noise [on the flight deck]." The visor had a thin heated gold film between the layers of glass to help demist the windows and give the pilots a clear view, thus preventing dazzle and acting as a shield to harmful ultraviolet and infrared radiation.

Concorde's droop nose and visor fully up for supersonic flight.
[© Vicentiu Ciorlaus]

Concorde's nose and visor lowered to 12.5° for approach/landing and taxiing.
[© David Apps]

Top: Concorde's visor up; bottom: Concorde's visor down.
[© Both images: © Jean-Philippe Lemaire]

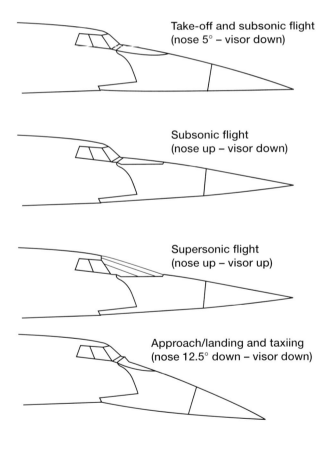

Take-off and subsonic flight
(nose 5° – visor down)

Subsonic flight
(nose up – visor down)

Supersonic flight
(nose up – visor up)

Approach/landing and taxiing
(nose 12.5° down – visor down)

To enhance Concorde's aerodynamic profile and protect the windscreen, a visor was raised which also cut the wind noise on the flight deck.
[© Suzanne O'Donoghue]

The Fuselage

At high speeds, Concorde's airframe got very hot. This heating was the result of friction between the outside air and the skin of the fast-moving aircraft. This caused the fuselage's metal to expand, thus allowing the aircraft to 'grow' by up to ten inches (25.5 cm). Every surface, even the windows, was warm to the touch even after landing. Therefore, it was a

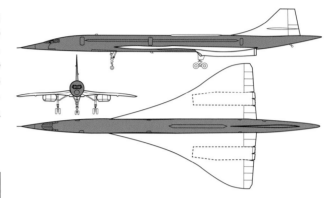

challenge for Concorde's designers to develop a fuselage and wings that were able to withstand the temperatures and pressures created by this high-speed environment. The changes in temperature caused the airframe's structures to expand and contract, so they were designed with intentional gaps and ways for various parts to move in relation to each other. Even the paint on the outside was flexible so that it could not flake off. Compared to subsonic airliners, Concorde had a thicker skin and extra reinforcements. The aircraft was built from a type of advanced aluminium alloy, enabling it to survive high tempera-

tures. Another challenge was how to ensure that windows could stand up to the heat and potential hazards of travelling at supersonic speeds when ordinary glazing would have shattered. Concorde's cabin windows are significantly smaller compared to the windows of subsonic aircraft. This would have reduced the speed of decompression in the event of a complete window failure while the flight crew could have made an emergency descent down to 15,000 feet (4,600 m). The glass for the cockpit and cabin (passenger) windows had to be tested at extremes that no civilian aircraft had ever experienced.

To minimize friction, Concorde's airframe had to be narrower and far more tapered at the front and back than subsonic airliners.
[© Adrian Meredith]

The Landing Gear

Philip Cairns who had been working on Concorde's landing gear, remembers what made set it apart from those of subsonic airliners:

"It consisted of four retractable pieces of undercarriage: the nose landing gear, two main landing gears and a tail bumper gear, all operated by the hydraulic system … Each of the two main landing gears had four wheels on their respective bogies. Each wheel had its own brake unit which was hydraulically operated and electrically controlled."

Patrick Sevestre, a former Air France Concorde ground engineer, further explains: "Both main gears retracted inwards into their bays and would be shortened by pulling the shock absorber up into their main bodies during the retraction process."

Philip Cairns: "The nose landing gear consisted of two wheels and would retract forward into its bay. Once all the gears were up and locked, the landing gear doors would shut."

Former flight engineer Ian Kirby adds: "The landing gear had to be long so that at touchdown, with the nose at high attitude, the backsides of the engines did not touch the ground.

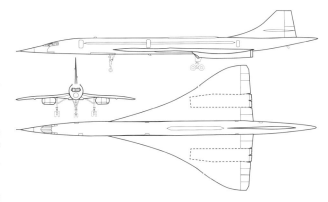

That was also the reason for the small tail bumper gear."

Philip Cairns: "You could get very dirty working on the undercarriages. We did numerous wheel and brake unit changes and used heavy lifting devices to accomplish these tasks at base which made it a bit easier. The main and nose landing gears were always fitted with ground locks when the aircraft arrived."

[© Bob Ware]

[© Dre Peijmen]

Concorde with fully extended landing gear. The left inset photo shows the tail bumper gear, the right a fully extended main gear. *[Large photo: © John Powell / johnnypowell.net]*

The Flight Deck

Although Concorde's flight deck (cockpit) looked very similar to those in subsonic airliners of the day, she featured several innovations as Philip Cairns explains:

"The flight controls were designed to be very accurate and robust. The elevons and rudders would be moved by the 4,000-psi hydraulic systems and controlled electrically, as well by a mechanical system which still used the hydraulics. They were organized in the following way: the 'Blue' system was the primary signalling system, next came 'Green' signalling, followed by the 'Mech' signalling. 'Mech' means mechanical which was levers, cables, cable tensioner, pulleys, rods, bell cranks, and a mixing chassis. 'Blue' and 'Green' signalling was purely electric wiring. More commonly known as fly-by-wire, I believe Concorde was the first civil airliner to have this system. The 'Blue' and 'Green' hydraulic systems provided the muscle to move the elevons and rudders, with 'Yellow' hydraulics being the backup. This in a nutshell was the control system that provided movement around the roll, yaw and pitch axis. It generally worked extremely well and was deemed a very reliable system for the performance that Concorde required."

Ian Kirby describes the fly-by-wire more in detail:

"... the signal from the pilot to the controls was by electrical signaling and a computer. The computer provided automatic stabilization about all three axis and lateral accelerometers to automatically correct for engine failure at high speed. The computer looked at what the pilot was requesting, looked at what the aircraft was doing, looked at where the flying controls were positioned and then decided how much to move each flying control surface. Concorde's flight deck was small and probably had more controls and dials than any other aircraft and many of the controls were multifunctional. The automatic landing system was

Concorde's flight deck with its analogue instruments. The captain's seat is at left, the co-pilot's (first officer) at right.
[© Bob Ware]

The rear part of the flight deck with the flight engineer's seat in the foreground. The jump seat for a guest is at left.
[© Air France Museum]

superb and gave us confidence that even in very adverse conditions it would put us safely on the ground in the middle of the runway. The flight simulator, or stimulator as it was often called, gave a reasonable representation of how the aircraft worked. It was nowhere near perfect but served us well for training and recurrent checks. There is no way a ground-based simulator can give the full feel of flight and definitely not the acceleration of a Concorde on take-off."

Philip Cairns describes the flight deck's layout:

"… it provided the pilots with brilliant forward views and seats that were powered up and down and forward and aft. They were powered because of emergencies and could be moved out of the way if necessary. The flight engineer also had a powered seat, and could move it to suit all inflight conditions, i.e. take-off or working his panel. He could also turn his seat through 90° to face forward. The flight deck had four seats available with another seat that could be used in the entrance to the flight deck, making a total of

five seats. The two additional seats were called 1st supernumerary seat and 2nd supernumerary seat. An interesting feature was the rearmost end of the engineer's panel; this is the place to be able to view and touch something remarkable. At Mach 2, Concorde is quite a warm aircraft and she can grow up to ten inches in length. At the end of the engineer's panel you can put your fingers in the gap there and move them back and forth. When the aircraft has landed and cooled down you cannot get your fingertips in the gap. The flight en-

gineer on one trip found that he was too hot during the flight, so he took his hat off and tucked it in this handy gap at the end of his panel. When Concorde landed in New York, he went to retrieve his hat but could not remove it as the aircraft had contracted and closed the gap."

Pilot Pierre Grange adds: "The flight control system allowed us to fly pleasantly manually all all speeds up to Mach 2. On one flight, André Turcat was on board and told us that he and his team had well taken care of this."

THE AGE OF CONCORDE

"It is a magnificent achievement that today British Airways are starting their first Concorde service. It is the outcome of fourteen years' close collaboration on design, production and testing between the British and French aircraft industries. I congratulate all those who have contributed to today's achievement and I wish every success to this beautiful aircraft now going into service."

– HM Queen Elizabeth II

Naming

In order to honour the Anglo-French cooperation which made a supersonic airliner possible in the first place, Timothy Clarke, the son of BAC Filton's publicity manager, suggested naming the aircraft 'Concorde', based on the French word *concorde* which has an English equivalent, *concord*. The meaning of both words is agreement, union, or harmony. After the British had changed it into 'Concord', the French put the 'e' back on, which resulted in an uproar in Britain. Finally, during the rollout of the Concorde prototype 001 in Toulouse in 1969, Tony Benn, Britain's Minister of Technology, made the announcement that the decision had been made to accept 'Concorde' as the official name but that the 'e' stood for *Excellence, England, Europe* and *Entente*, thus able to pacify the critics who did not want to see the French 'e' on the aircraft.

During her development Concorde's designers and engineers overcame numerous technological challenges but costs spiralled to about five times the initial estimate. During the early 1970s, while the general public in France and Britain was still showing keen interest in the 'airliner of the future', the British parliament began expressing concerns over the project's soaring expense, and even began considering a cancellation of the entire project. However, the Anglo-French agreement included a clause that if either side wanted to cancel the programme this gave the other party the right to claim damages. Therefore, it was speculated that the possible financial burden of cancelling could have been bigger than the costs of continuing. Despite the escalating costs the two nations decided to resolve their differences and carry on.

An Air France flight attendant advertises the age of supersonic air travel.
[© Air France]

Sales Tours

While still being used for test flights, both France and Britain sent their prototypes on demonstration and sales tours around the world in order to attract more potential buyers. In 1971 the French-built Concorde 001 made her first transatlantic flight via the Cape Verde islands, Cayenne and Sao Paolo, finally arriving in Rio de Janeiro where she received a warm welcome and made several demonstration flights.

During the following year, Philip Cairns, who would later become a Concorde ground engineer at British Airways, participated in the British sales tour of Iran, India, Singapore, Japan and Australia: "I was very fortunate to be chosen to go on this fantastic trip. There were many highlights for me including my first and second flight on Concorde, the first one from Tehran to Bahrain and the second from Beirut to Toulouse in

France. Prototype 002 was the real star of this wonderful trip as she showed the world what she could do. Everywhere we went the public were very receptive; the press reports were understandably mixed as they tried to find the right words to describe this new 'Queen of the Skies'."

Although Concorde had overcome the Anglo-French budgetary disagreements and was admired by people from

around the world, the project suffered several blows. Concorde's sonic boom made supersonic air travel overland practically impossible without causing complaints from people, thus ruining her unique selling point, particularly in the United States. Moreover, various events further dampened Concorde sales prospects. One of them was the 1973 oil crisis that resulted in soaring fuel prices. Many air-

Prototype 002 overflies Singapore during the 1972 sales tour.
[© British Airways]

Sonic Boom

An aircraft travelling through the air produces sound waves. If it is travelling slower than the speed of sound (Mach 1), then sound waves can propagate ahead of the aircraft. If the vehicle breaks the sound barrier, thus flying faster than the speed of sound, it produces a sonic boom. This boom is the 'wake' of the aircraft's sound waves. All of the sound waves that would have normally propagated ahead of the plane are compressed to form one shockwave so at first you hear nothing, and then you hear the boom they create. Concorde produces a double boom: the front pressure cone produces the first boom, and then as the aircraft tail passes through this pressure cone the air shockwaves go back to normal, which produces the second boom. You then get the double boom, which sounds like boom boom.

lines which had previously shown interest in operating Concorde now become very cautious about aircraft types with a significantly higher fuel consumption than subsonic airliners. Another devastating event was the introduction of new wide-body aircraft, most notably the Boeing 747 which began her operational service in 1970. Airliners like her made subsonic commercial air travel far more cost-efficient for the airlines. The Boeing 747 could transport three times more passengers than Concorde, was much more fuel-efficient, and had a much wider range, being capable of flying to nearly every destination across the globe including overland routes. In such times of economic uncertainty, the 747 looked like a significantly less risky investment. Therefore, one airline after another which had placed (non-binding) orders for Concorde cancelled them.

With several production aircraft already under construction and no buyers in sight, Concorde's future looked bleak. Both Britain and France, which had invested in a project whose ambition at the time was second only to the American and Soviet space programmes, now looked at their national airlines. British Airways and Air France, then still state-owned, appeared to be the only two potential operators for Concorde. Therefore, the British and French governments decided to 'sell' the Concordes then under construction to both airlines, which actually meant that British Airways and Air France got their aircraft basically for free. Therefore, the price to develop and build Concorde was completely paid for by British and French taxpayers. Eventually, both airlines would each operate a fleet of seven Concordes.

The official handover of the first Concorde to British Airways on 15 January 1976 at Heathrow Airport.
[© Steven Fitzgerald]

Supersonic Rivals

Nigel Ferris, contributing editor to the Mach 2 Concorde magazine, takes a look at Concorde's competitors from both the United States and the Soviet Union: "The Anglo-French Government agreement to build a supersonic transport (SST) was signed on the 29th November 1962. At about the same time, the Soviets and Americans both decided to proceed with their own SSTs, and design contracts were issued for those proposals. In the Soviet Union Tupolev gained this authority, while in the United States Boeing and Lockheed began their studies, namely the Boeing 2707 and Lockheed L-2000.

Boeing 2707

"The American victor was Boeing. Their original design was for a Mach 3 swing-wing aircraft, for 250–300 passengers. This was considerably bigger than Concorde, and would have been the longest aircraft ever produced, and as envisaged would have been able to supercruise at Mach 3. In order to achieve such a feat, the aircraft would have had to have been made primarily of titanium, able to withstand the high temperatures over the airframe – as a result of the airflow over the structure undergoing compression. By contrast, the maximum temperature allowed for Concorde at Mach 2 at the pitot tube on the nose was 127°C. Titanium, however, is more difficult to machine than Concorde's aluminium alloy, and much more expensive. Concorde, however, did use some titanium, as a firewall in each nacelle between the paired engines. The Boeing 2707 would have had full-length leading-edge slats and trailing-edge flaps. The complexity of designing and manufacturing hinge and pivot points for the swing wings, their ability to withstand supersonic cruise, and their strength (and cost) led Boeing to revert to a more conventional fixed-wing design. However, due to cost and other factors, the project was cancelled in 1971. The swing-wing concept is not uncommon. Examples of supersonic aircraft with swing wings include the European multirole aircraft Panavia Tornado, the American bombers Rockwell B1A and B1B Lancer, as well as the former Soviet bomber Tupolev Tu-160."

Cockpit section and droop nose of the Boeing 2707 mock-up on display at the Museum of Flight, Seattle.
[© Ted Huetter, Museum of Flight] Inset: Drawing of the Boeing 2707.

The Tupolev Tu-144

"The Tu-144 (NATO code-name 'Charger') first flew on 31 December 1968 – beating Concorde's first flight on 2 March 1969. It is well documented that this was a lesser design than Concorde, however; at the time there were stories of industrial espionage whereby the British and French allowed 'doctored' blueprints to be passed on, resulting in this flawed design. Various differences from Concorde were readily observable. The wing shape did not include the complex curves and cambers of Concorde's design. The main undercarriage had six main wheels per bogie, as opposed to just four on Concorde – this was due to superior tyre and brake technology on the part of Britain and France. The Tu-144 prototypes utilized afterburning turbofans, which meant, due to the size, higher induced nacelle aerodynamic drag. Later models – after much redesign – featured efficient 'canards' on the nose behind the cockpit to improve low-speed handling characteristics, repositioned engine nacelles, and undercarriage retraction. The Tu-144 had to employ partial reheat to maintain supersonic cruise (supercruise is defined as maintaining supersonic speed without reheat). Concorde employed twin spool axial flow turbojets, with computer-controlled intakes, throttle amplifiers, primary and secondary nozzles, without the need for continued reheat. The aircraft went into service, but only completed 102 flights in total: fifty-five as passenger-carrying, the rest as cargo. Whether her non-success was due to design, lack of profitability, or 'espionage' will never be fully known. The Tu-144 occupies a special place in aviation, as does the Boeing design – although the latter was only ever seen as a wooden mock-up."

"At the Paris Air Show in 1973, both Concorde and the Tu-144 were on show. The French Air Force sent up one of their fighters to photograph the aircraft showing the 'canards'. As a result of the French fighter flying too close to the Tu-144, the Soviet pilot had to take emergency action to avoid collision, putting the aircraft into a pitch-down attitude. This resulted in a surge in all four engines, leading to flame-out, so the pilot initiated a further downward pitch attitude in an attempt to windmill-start the engines. This failed, and as a result the Tu-144 went into a 1g negative dive. This overloaded the structural integrity of the aircraft, and the left outer wing broke off, causing the aircraft to crash."

Concorde on display at the Paris Air Show in 1973 with the Tupolev Tu-144 still on the ground. When the latter performed later that day it crashed without any survivors.
[© Aris Pappas]

In order to beat Concorde, the Tupolev Tu-144's design was rushed. However, she flew three months before Concorde. To this day, she holds the speed record as the fastest supersonic airliner with a top speed of Mach 2.35.
[© Aris Pappas]

Although the Tu-144 (right) had a droop nose like Concorde (left), it did not have a retractable visor.
[© Tu-144: Jim Ross, NASA / Concorde: British Airways]

The Inaugural Commercial Flights

BRITISH AIRWAYS and AIR FRANCE

request the pleasure of your company at a
reception in the Tavern in the Sky restaurant,
Terminal Three, Heathrow Airport, London,
before the departure of Concorde
on its first commercial service.
Wednesday, 21st January 1976.

RSVP
Chief of Information Services
Public Relations · British Airways
Victoria Terminal
Buckingham Palace Road, SW1

RECEPTION 10 a.m. · PLEASE BRING THIS CARD WITH YOU

Invitation to Concorde's inaugural commercial flight. *[© British Airways]*

At 11:40 on 21 January 1976 aviation saw a giant leap forward when Air France Concorde F-BVFA and British Airways Concorde G-BOAA lifted off at the same instant, thus inaugurating Concorde's commercial service life. It had taken more than twenty years to make this memorable day happen. Both aircraft were the first of their fleets to be fully prepared for commercial service. F-BVFA had made her maiden flight on 27 October 1975 and had been delivered to Air France six weeks later. G-BOAA had first flown on 5 November 1975 and was delivered to British Airways in January 1976. Prior to her maiden commercial flight, Concorde had received praise from various people:

"Soon there will only be two breeds of airlines – those who have Concorde and those who have not ... We are confident of filling up our Concordes."

"I look forward to introducing the Concorde into service and making a success of it, and I am sure it will be."

– M. Pierre Giraudet, President of Air France

– David Nicolson, Chairman of British Airways

Concorde personnel from both airlines worked closely together to coordinate the departures so that the two aircraft could take off simultaneously. A telephone link was set up between the control towers at Charles de Gaulle and Heathrow airports, where the air traffic controllers would give a thirty-second countdown over a special frequency. Norman Todd, captain of G-BOAA (flight BA300), and Pierre Chanoine, commanding F-BVFA (flight AF085) and soon-to-be captain, would release their aircraft's brakes at exactly the same instant to begin their take-off roll and would stay in touch as their aircraft were being pushed back. While the Concorde crews carried out their pre-departure checks, the first passengers, including fee-paying passengers, press and VIPs, assembled in the departure lounge. Watched by more than 200 million television viewers around the world, both Concordes began to roll, accompanied by the distinctive sound of the four powerful Olympus engines. As both aircraft flawlessly took off and began retracting their undercarriages, the age of supersonic air travel became a reality.

Ian Kirby, who later became a senior flight officer on board Concorde, experienced G-BOAA's take-off from a carpark at Heathrow:

"I watched as 'AA started to accelerate, initially in

G-BOAA taking off for her inaugural commercial flight to Bahrain. Note the Pan Am Boeing 707 in the background – carrying Kathy Rhodes who later shared how she experienced this significant moment in aviation history.
[© Adrian Meredith]

near silence. It took a few seconds for the sound to travel from those powerful Olympus engines to my location. When the sound did arrive it was like no other aircraft. Perhaps the nearest was the VC-10, which also had an exhaust that was supersonic. G-BOAA came past with a very satisfying roar and a faint yellow/brown haze from the exhaust. The rotation seemed fairly slow but 'AA was soon airborne, initially at a fairly gentle angle and then at a much increased angle and a very rapid rate of climb. I noticed the haze of the

exhaust change to a much darker colour and saw the glow of the reheats subside as they were selected off and power reduced. At the same time the aircraft reduced its pitch attitude and continued at a reduced rate of climb. It took a while for the sound reduction to be evident in the carpark, but I am sure those living under the flight path appreciated the reduction sooner. Suddenly it was nearly all over as 'AA merged into the distance. The aircraft turned south and then east as it was bound for Bahrain. From the carpark we could see and just hear it in the

distance, but soon it was gone. So it was back home to watch it all again on the evening news."

Kathy Rhodes, who worked as a senior purser on a Pan Am flight from London to Boston, witnessed G-BOAA's take-off for Concorde's inaugural flight from her Boeing 707 at Heathrow:

"It was a routine morning: standard transport to the airport, briefing, boarding, and taxiing for take-off. Near the end of our taxi we halted. We sat for a while. I was about to check with the cockpit when the captain came on

Captain Norman Todd (centre), Captain Brian Calvert (right) and Senior Engineer Officer John Lidiard on G-BOAA's maiden British Airways flight to Bahrain on 21 January 1976. Air France's inaugural flight crew consisted of Captain Pierre Dudal, the airline's chief Concorde pilot, soon-to-be Captain Pierre Chanoine and Chief Flight Engineer André Blanc. *[© British Airways]*

the PA and announced the reason for the delay. We were second behind Concorde for take-off and had to wait for clearance. The plan was for the French Concorde to take off from Paris at the same time the British were to take off from London's Heathrow airport. The French were running late. I left my jump seat and looked out both sides of our 707, the aircraft that brought jet travel to the world. There wasn't any view of the Concorde from either side, but I could see the Royal Family lined up along the tarmac to witness this historic take-off. I went up to the cockpit and from there had a wonderful view of this sleek, modern supersonic jet that was bringing new horizons to the world. I asked the captain if he could manoeuvre our plane so that our passengers could see Concorde. He obliged, angling the aircraft so Concorde was visible out the right side. We let our passengers roam the cabin to get a good view, before we had to buckle in for take-off. We could not see Concorde take off from the cabin, but the roar of those mighty engines could be felt throughout. What an exhilarating experience – and our passengers were all thrilled to be part of it."

British Airways G-BOAA went supersonic 1 hour

and 20 minutes after her take-off, as she flew out over the Adriatic Sea, before reaching Mach 2. She passed over Lebanon, Syria and Saudi Arabia, then down the Gulf to land at Bahrain at 15:17 GMT – just 3 hours and 37 minutes after beginning her take-off roll at Heathrow. Ali Janahi recalls her arrival:

"I remember the first Concorde flight was to Bahrain, and that made Bahrain well known to the world. Whenever I spoke to people in Europe, Asia or anywhere else, they asked me where I was from. When I said Bahrain, even though most people had no clue where Bahrain was, they immediately recognized the name as the first country where Concorde flew. So in a sense it was great PR for Bahrain."

When the British Airways Concorde landed at Bahrain, Kathy Rhodes was midway across the Atlantic on her flight to Boston in her Pan Am Boeing 707:

"The flight engineer noted that if we'd been on Concorde, we'd be there by now. Since this was prior to reasonable duty limits for cabin crew, my response was that if we'd been on Concorde, we might well be on our way back by now."

Meanwhile, Air France Concorde F-BVFA completed her much longer flight, from Paris to Dakar in Senegal and then across the Atlantic to Rio de Janeiro in Brazil, finally arriving at 19:00. As evening fell, the world passed into a new era of speed and style, allowing ordinary people to fly faster and higher than most military pilots, while enjoying the best luxury service both airlines could provide. His Excellency Faisal al Mutawa, Kuwait's ambassador to France, praised Concorde with the following words:

"She is undoubtedly a very impressive aircraft which could perfectly fit in a multinational Arab airline. Remarkable by its safety and speed, Concorde is indeed the expression of the genius of France and Great Britain."

British airways

welcome you aboard

their

first Concorde service

Bahrain — London

22nd January, 1976

Aperitifs & Cocktails

Sweet and Dry Vermouth
Campari Soda
Americano . Negroni
Medium Dry Sherry
Dry Martini . Gin . Vodka
Bloody Mary . Old Fashioned . Manhattan
Sours – Whisky . Gin . Brandy
Gin Fizz

Highballs – Whisky . Brandy . Gin . Rum

Champagne Cocktail

Spirits

Whisky – Scotch . Bourbon . Rye
Gin
Vodka

Beers

Ale . Lager

Selection of Soft Drinks

Wines

Champagne
Dom Perignon 1969
Bordeaux
Château Brane Cantenac 1970
Burgundy
Chablis-Laroche et fils 1973

Aperitifs — Champagne

Caviar and smoked salmon canapés

Lunch

Cold breast of chicken with foie gras
and asparagus spears

*

Mixed green salad with
vinaigrette dressing

*

Assorted cheeses

*

Poached orange in grand marnier

*

Coffee

*

Remy Martin Napoleon brandy
Drambuie . Cointreau

*

Havana cigars

Menu for the first flight from Bahrain back to London on 22 January 1976. *[© British Airways]*

Scheduled Flights

Advertisement announcing Air France's commercial Concorde service.
[© Air France Museum]

Mach 2: Jour J.
21 janvier 1976, Concorde effectue le premier vol commercial supersonique de l'histoire.

cause of Concorde's sonic boom. Without New York, there weren't too many lucrative destinations left to which Concorde could fly. Also, many New Yorkers demonised Concorde not only for her sonic boom, her noisy engines but also for environmental issues. During the early 1970s the environmental lobby was becoming increasingly vocal, expressing the concern that the exhausts of a global fleet of hundreds of supersonic airliners flying at 60,000 feet could do extreme damage to the ozone layer.

On 21 January 1976 British Airways began its commercial service on the London–Bahrain route and Air France on its Paris–Rio de Janeiro (via Dakar) route. The Paris–Caracas route (via the Azores) began in April. With New York still closed to Concorde, the US Secretary of Transportation, William Coleman, gave her permission to fly to Washington Dulles International Airport. Both airlines simultaneously began a thrice-weekly service to Dulles in May 1976. However, due to low demand, Air France cancelled its Washington service in October 1982, while British Airways continued it until November 1994. In February 1977 Secretary Coleman lifted the US ban of New York's John F. Kennedy Airport: "I have de-

cided for the reasons set forth in detail in the opinion to permit British Airways and Air France to conduct limited schedule commercial flights into the United States."

Although New York had banned Concorde locally, that ban came to an end on 17 October 1977 when the US Supreme Court finally decided in favour of Concorde. Despite numerous noise complaints, the noise report concluded that several subsonic aircraft, including the US President's Air Force One, then a Boeing 707, was actually louder than Concorde during take-off and landing and at subsonic speeds. Scheduled service from Paris and London to New York began on 22 November 1977. Within minutes of each other, French and

Flight attendant Nicole Méneveux disembarking Concorde Fox Delta (F-BVFD) after the historic flight to New York on 22 November 1977.
[© Nicole Méneveux]

After Concorde had received her certificate of airworthiness in 1975, British Airways and Air France set their sights on the US east coast, in particular New York as it was considered the number one destination for Concorde's future business travellers. However, the US Congress had just

banned Concorde landings in the United States, officially due to citizen protest over sonic booms, so preventing Concorde flying the most coveted route across the Atlantic. Moreover, large countries such as India and Australia refused to grant Concorde overflying rights be-

British Airways and Air France Concordes at Washington Dulles International Airport in May 1976.
[© Adrian Meredith]

British Concordes landed at John F. Kennedy Airport. Fifteen years after signing the Anglo-French 'Entente Concordiale', Concorde had finally triumphed over one of her major odds.

Nicole Méneveux worked as a Concorde flight attendant for Air France from 1976 to 1992. Cherishing these sixteen years as the best time of her career, she recalls the first commercial Concorde flight from Paris to New York: "This day was a memorable day in the history of commercial aviation, and I had the opportunity to participate in the event. Before take-off, I was very excited but we had to stay focused to offer a perfect service as we were carrying our minister of transport, Air France's general manager, business leaders, the press, and about thirty passengers realizing their dreams of flying Concorde. We were very impressed by the presence of a grand eighty-one-year-old gentleman: aviation pioneer Maurice Bellonte who had performed the first west-bound crossing of the North Atlantic, from Paris to New York, in a Breguet XIX in 1930. Monsieur Bellonte had witnessed such vast progress in aviation technology since his memorable flight. The take-off was very emotional and we were literally glued to our seats. By 11:22 we had reached a height of 28,000

Advertisement for Air France's service from Paris to Rio de Janeiro.
[© Air France Museum]

Advertisement for British Airways' service from London to Singapore.
[© British Airways]

feet [8,500m] and as we passed the Normandy coast we enjoyed a breathtaking view of the cliffs at Étretat on one side and La Pointe du Hoc, where the U.S. Rangers had landed during the Allied invasion on 6 June 1944, on the other. We then accelerated to Mach 2 and served the meals prepared by the master chefs.

"After going into our descent we landed three minutes later than scheduled in order to land exactly in the same moment as the British Airways Concorde which was making its first flight from London to New York that day. It was a sublime moment when the two white birds majestically rolled toward each other on the tarmac and met nose to nose, as if kissing, in front of the Big Apple. I had tears in my eyes and I wasn't the only one. We finally had won the battle against all the noise protesters and

British Airways Concorde Alpha Delta (G-BOAD) painted in Singapore Airlines livery on her port side and in British Airways livery on her starboard side.
[© Aris Pappas]

contrary to what had been announced - and what we feared - there were no Concorde opponents waiting to throw tomatoes at us. So, was this just another routine day for Concorde? No, it was the first commercial flight from Paris to New York."

Although the Concordes of both airlines were identical, there was one other critical distinction as Frank Debouck points out: "The essential difference was the shorter distance between London and New York than between Paris and New York. Therefore, the flight for the British was a little bit easier than for the French as each transatlantic Concorde flight was considered 'short on fuel'. British Airways had two daily flights to New York, Air France had only one."

In 1977, British Airways and Singapore Airlines shared Concorde Alpha Delta (G-BOAD) for commercial flights between London and Singapore via Bahrain. This route was an extension of the existing London–Bahrain route. Alpha Delta was painted in British Airways livery on her starboard side and in Singapore Airlines livery on her port side. After a dispute with the Indian government in which Concorde was not allowed to fly at supersonic speeds in Indian airspace, the route was eventually declared not lucrative and therefore discontinued in 1980.

Between 1978 and 1982 Air France operated a

Concorde check-in in 1978. British oil tycoon Fred Finn receives his ticket. With 718 flights, he is the most-travelled Concorde passenger. Pascal Le Borgne, a French businessman, logged more than 400 trips to become Air France's most frequent Concorde flyer.
[© British Airways]

Concorde service twice weekly to Mexico City via Washington, DC, or New York City. The worldwide economic crisis during that period, however, resulted in the discontinuation of this route as the last flights were almost empty. The flight from Washington or New York and Mexico City included a deceleration (from Mach 2.02 to Mach 0.95) in order to enable Concorde to overfly Florida subsonically and avoid creating the (prohibited) sonic boom. When the aircraft

On 18 October 1982, two Concordes, one from Air France, and the other from British Airways, made a dual simultaneous landing at Orlando International Airport. This was a publicity stunt organized by Disney World to hype the arrival of the sponsors of exhibits at Disney's newly opened Epcot Center's British and French pavilions.
[© Adrian Meredith]

Musicians welcome an Air France Concorde in Mexico City.
[© Air France Museum]

reached the open water to cross the Gulf of Mexico she could re-accelerate back to supersonic speeds. In 1978 the US airline Braniff International Airways began leasing various Concordes for subsonic flights between Dallas Fort Worth and Washington Dulles International Airport, flown by Braniff flight crews. Air France and British Airways crews then took over for the continuing supersonic transatlantic flights to London and Paris. With these flights generating no profit Braniff was forced to end its operation as the only US Concorde operator in 1980. From 1984 to 1991 British Airways Concordes operated a thrice-weekly service between London and Miami via Washington Dulles. From 1987 to 2003, during the summer and winter holiday season, British Airways flew once a week to Grantley Adams International Airport in Barbados in the Caribbean.

Charter Flights

During the 1980s, British Airways and Air France had to look for new ways to make Concorde more profitable and to secure her operational future as her early years had not proven economically viable. The only regular route she could fly successfully was the transatlantic route from either London or Paris to New York or Washington and back. To make the best out of this route, Concorde's marketing teams decided to make her very exclusive and put up the prices in order to generate sustainable profits. With some of the aircraft often sitting idle in London or Paris, it became possible to charter Concorde – now anyone with the money could now hire a whole Concorde and take her wherever they wanted.

For many ordinary people in France and Britain, whose tax money had helped to build Concorde, flying with her became a reality as the ticket prices for an one-hour supersonic flight experience ('supersonic loops') only cost a fraction of the transatlantic round ticket. The charter market exploded as entrepreneurs, Concorde fan clubs, and travel agents cashed in on the new demand. Those charter flights took Concorde to over 350 destinations around the world, thus enabling Concorde to be used for the trip of a lifetime.

Frank Debouck remembers: "In addition to the regular flights to New York, I developed numerous charter flights – these included supersonic looks taking off from Paris, the 1999 speed world tour, promotional events including the Pepsi flight, many prestigious around-the-world tours as well as exotic destinations such as the Arctic Circle, Ushuaia, Easter Island, or Santiago de Chile. All in all we flew to more than 150 destinations on charter flights with Air France Concordes. During these flight, many personal encounters left quite an impression on me, including a very unique flight with fifty British children and their fifty grandmothers to meet Santa Claus in northern Finland. Both Air France and British Airways often made numerous charter flights for the same customers and we were very respectful of each other."

For many enthusiasts, Concorde herself become the destination. This innovative and lucrative use of Concorde became a major marketing tool for both Air France and British Airways. Pierre Grange, a former Air France Concorde co-pilot remembers his charter flights: "I flew Concorde from 1984 and 1989, at a

British Airways and Air France certificates confirming a supersonic flight aboard Concorde.
[© British Airways / Air France Museum]

During Concorde's twenty-seven years of commercial service, there were only two female pilots – Barbara Harmer (left) for British Airways, and Béatrice Vialle (right) for Air France.
[Left: © British Airways / Right: © Béatrice Vialle]

time when charter flights were numerous and very different. They ranged from the 'supersonic loops' to 21-day world tours with a wealthy clientele. At the time there were also the presidential flights as François Mitterrand always used Concorde for his state visits. All these charter flights were very special compared to regular flights as the passengers were extremely enthusiastic and we flew to unusual places for Air France such as Bali, Sydney, Las Vegas, or Kathmandu."

Special Flights

Besides carrying heads of state and business leaders, Concorde sometimes made special flights for demonstrations, and air shows such as the Farnborough, Paris-Le Bourget, and Oshkosh AirVenture, as well as national parades and celebrations in France and Britain. The aircraft were also used for advertising purposes (including for Pepsi), for Olympic torch relays (XVI. Winter Olympic Games in Albertville, France, 1992) and for observing solar eclipses (including 1973 and 1999).

Records

Concorde not only looked like a record-breaking aircraft promising speed, she also delivered numerous records in civil aviation. On 13 February 1985, a Concorde charter flight flew from London Heathrow to Sydney, Australia, in 17 hours, 3 minutes and 45 seconds, including refuelling stops.

Concorde also set the official 'Westbound Around the World' as well as the 'Eastbound Around the World' world air speed records. On 12–13 October 1992, commemorating the 500th anniversary of Columbus' landing in the New World, the US-based charter firm Concorde Spirit Tours chartered Air France's Sierra Delta (F-BTSD) and circumnavigated the world in 32 hours, 49 minutes and 3 seconds, from Lisbon, Portugal. This westbound record flight included six refuelling stops at Santo Domingo, Acapulco, Honolulu, Guam, Bangkok, and Bahrain. On 15–16 August 1995, Sierra Delta also set the eastbound record under Concorde Spirit Tours charter. This promotional flight circumnavigated the world from New York John F. Kennedy International Airport in 31 hours, 27 minutes 49 seconds. This flight included six refuelling stops at Toulouse, Dubai, Bangkok, Andersen Air Force Base on Guam, Honolulu, and Acapulco.

On 7 February 1996 British Airways' Alpha Delta (G-BOAD) made the fastest transatlantic airliner flight from New York JFK to London Heathrow in just 2 hours, 52 minutes and 59 seconds from take-off to touchdown (aided by a 175 mph or 282 kph tailwind).

On 2 March 1999, exactly thirty years after her maiden flight in 1969, Concorde had flown 920,000 hours, with more than 600,000 supersonic – many more than all of the other supersonic aircraft in the Western world combined. On her final flight to the Museum of Flight in November 2003, British Airways' Alpha Golf (G-BOAG) set a New York City–Seattle speed record of 3 hours, 55 minutes and 12 seconds. Due to the restrictions on supersonic flights over US territory, the Canadian authorities granted Concorde permission to overfly sparsely populated Canadian territory for the majority of the journey.

Concorde flying at twice the speed of sound – Mach 2.
[© Gérard Duval]

In comparison: the early British Airways Mach meter (top), and the latest Mach meter in use until 2003.
[© Left: © Adrian Meredith / Right: © Johnathan Safford]

The Captain's Eye View

"What pilot – from the flyer of a light aircraft to the most braid-decked jetliner captain – has not dreamed of one day piloting Concorde? Some of us have realized this dream: Concorde is our field marshal's baton. To those who are still hoping for the day when they will fly Concorde, we can say that this is a fantastic machine with a revolutionary wing which will bring them, too, new sensations and the same feeling of pride at taking a giant step up the ladder of speed."

– Pierre Dudal, former AF Concorde chief pilot

A supersonic journey between London and New York, as seen from a Concorde flight deck, was described by Captain Andrew, general manager, flight technical services, British Airways, in 1977:

Concorde pilots during their regular simulator training, 1970s. Over time, these machines become more sophisticated.
[© Air France Museum]

"The highly experienced British Airways crews chosen to fly Concorde have to go back to school before they can operate this beautiful supersonic aircraft in service. Each crew consists of a captain, who has probably been flying for about twenty-five years, a co-pilot and a flight engineer.

They spend two to three months on Concorde conversion courses at the airline's Technical Training Centre. The crews learn how to manage the aircraft and its equipment safely and efficiently, and how to identify and deal with malfunctions. This usually involves no more than switching over to a standby system – most are duplicated and many are triplicated.

The next stage is the flight simulator – a Concorde in every respect but one. It never leaves the ground. Here the picture comes together. The simulator is 'flown' to New York, Tokyo, or anywhere in the world, while problems of every kind are thrown in and dealt with.

Only when the coveted 'Concorde' endorsements are entered in their licences are the pilots and flight engineers qualified to operate on the routes. But they will still be under supervision until British Airways is satisfied that each has sufficient experience to operate on his own.

About ninety minutes before take-off, the captain and crew check the proposed routing in the briefing room. The weather at destination – say New York – is forecast to be cloudy, with a lowish ceiling of 300 feet and poor visibility of one mile for arrival. This is no problem at all with the dual autopilot that will land the aircraft safely in much worse conditions. Weather at Montreal is good.

London has a westerly wind and Runway 28 left will be used for take-off. The noise abatement procedure is studied and the captain looks again at the route. Climb at subsonic speed to Hartland Point, then accelerate and climb to 51,000 feet on route 'Alpha', which runs south of Ireland and Newfoundland, and then reduce speed some 350 miles from New York. A climbing cruise is planned to save fuel – normal fuel reserves allowing diversion from New York to Montreal are available – and there is a full load of passengers.

Concorde showing her graceful lines. Photos like this were used as a backdrop for advertising images promoting exclusive automobiles such as the BMW M1 in 1978.
[© Air France]

The fuel figure is confirmed and the crew leaves for the aircraft to begin the checks. While the flight engineer supervises fuelling, the co-pilot begins a systematic check of the aircraft systems. Soon the engineer returns to the flight deck to carry out his part of the check. Meanwhile the captain has loaded the en-route waypoints into the three inertial navigation systems (INSs). Each inertial system has its own very accurate gyros and accelerometers that detect any movement of the aircraft. These movements are passed as signals to the three INS computers that calculate automatically speed and track, wind effect, and the aircraft's position to a tenth of a mile.

When the captain loads into each INS computer the latitude and longitude of the various points along the route, the computers cal-culate swiftly the required track and the distance and time to that point. They provide a signal to the pilots' instruments which show whether the aircraft is right or left of track, and to the autopilot, so that the aircraft flies automatically from one waypoint to the next.

The captain will also set up conventional radio aids for the first part of his departure. He knows that he can expect a Brecon One departure – the standard routing to the west – "Climb straight ahead after take-off to pick up the 263° bearing of the London VOR (radio direction-finding beacon) and, at seven miles' range from London DME [distance-measuring equipment], turn right to Woodley beacon and make good a track of 275°. Cross Woodley at 4,000 feet."

The passengers are boarding and the weight and balance sheet is brought to the captain. Doors are closed and the first engine is started. It is 11 a.m. in London and you are due in New York in three hours forty minutes – at 9.40 a.m. New York time.

Once all checks are completed and cleared for take-off on the runway, the captain opens the throttles and releases the brakes. Four green lights tell the crew that reheat is operating. This provides extra power. Your feel the tremendous thrust as the four powerful engines accelerate the aircraft swiftly and smoothly down the runway. At 200 mph [320 kph] the captain begins to raise the nose and at 230 mph [370 kph] the aircraft leaves the ground and climbs away.

Acceleration is rapid and the initial noise abatement speed of 290 mph [465 kph] is reached as soon as the co-pilot has raised the wheels. Climbing rapidly at this speed, the captain calls for climb power before the first houses are reached. This reduces community noise effectively while providing an adequate and safe climb. Over Woodley radio beacon at 4,000 feet, the air traffic controller clears the aircraft to climb to 26,000 feet to Hartland Point.

The visor is raised. There is an amazing noise cut-off when this is done and the flight deck becomes very quiet. Speed is increased to 460 mph [735 kph] for the climb. The captain selects the autopilot – 26,000 feet on the automatic height capture – 400 knots on the airspeed hold – INS guidance – and Concorde is on its way with fully automatic control, but always under the watchful eye of the crew.

Passing the coast, clearance is received to accel-

At 200 mph [320 kph] the captain begins to raise the nose and at 230 mph [370 kph] Concorde leaves the ground and climbs away with rapid acceleration.
[© Art Brett]

erate and climb to 51,000 feet. The flight engineer has already begun to transfer some fuel to the rear trim tank to compensate for the movement of the centre of lift as speed increases.

At 26,000 feet and cruising at Mach 0.93, the captain increases power. Almost immediately you are through Mach 1 – the speed of sound – and beginning the climb. In the cabin the passengers will notice nothing as Concorde passes Mach 1. Concorde moves effortlessly into supersonic speed, to the mode of flight for which it was designed and where it performs so beautifully.

Once supersonic, the flight becomes rock steady. Disturbances are left behind as you climb well above the clouds into the stratosphere. The sky takes on that darker hue familiar to astronauts. Far below, the subsonic airliners are moving out on their eight-hour flight to New York. Concorde swiftly passes each one and is soon 500 miles from London, starting the climbing cruise at Mach 2. The high speed has heated the nose and leading edges of the wings to 125°C. Outside the passenger windows the surface temperature is 100°C, but when you touch

a window it is cool. Climbing slowly as weight reduces, the aircraft reaches the deceleration point 350 miles from New York and now at a height of 58,000 feet.

New York weather is still fairly misty, but this presents no problem. Throttle back and the Concorde descends towards the Deer Park radio facility, where all New York procedures begin. Fifteen minutes later the New York controller has instructed the aircraft to leave Deer Park, heading 210° for a landing on Runway 4 right.

The final radios are set and checked. 'Land' mode

is selected on the autopilot. As you join the ILS [instrument landing system] radio beam, the captain calls: "Gear down – landing check." The nose and visor have been lowered to give good vision during the approach and the autopilot steers the aircraft accurately down the beam, watched carefully by the crew.

Over the threshold, throttles close for a fully automatic landing. Gently select reverse thrust and brakes, then taxi in to the BA terminal only three hours forty minutes after leaving London."

A Concorde captain and a member of the ground staff chat after the aircraft's arrival. The relationship between Concorde's crew and the ground staff was very close.
[© British Airways]

Mach 2 Passenger

by Ben Wang, United States

*"We flew faster than the sun and I
gained an extra hour in my life!"*

Being a child of the 1970s and interested in aviation, it was hard not to notice Concorde. Who wouldn't want to fly on her? I always wanted to. When Concorde's retirement was announced in April 2003, I told myself I had to fly on her … it was now or never. In early May, I booked the special one-way World Traveller economy Concorde ticket for 1 July.

After arriving at London Heathrow Airport I entered the British Airways Lounge Pavilion to check in for my flight. From the Concorde Room I then went downstairs to the Molton Brown Spa. A shower room was instantly available and after a shower, a back massage (with Pam) followed; it was so relaxing that I thought I was going to fall asleep. At the bar I ordered a Chinese prawn salad and then grabbed a table. When our aircraft, Alpha Golf (G-BO-AG), arrived at 16:50, there

The e-ticket receipt for Ben Wang's flight on Concorde. In comparison: in 1977, the one-way fare from London to New York was £430, in 2003 it was £4,600.
[© All photos: © Ben Wang]

```
BRITISH AIRWAYS          DUPLICATE          CPN 01 OF 01
                E-TICKET RECEIPT / ITINERARY  DATE:08MAY04
ENDORSEMENTS:NO CASH REF                      ISSUED BY:33993466
                                             TBA
                                             BRITISH AIRWAYS
NAME:WANG/BEN MR
BOOKING REF:YFMZ6K
FROM                    TO                 FLIGHT  CL DATE   TIME ST BAG
NEW YORK       JFK LONDON          LHR BA  174 M 17JUN 1900 OK 2PC
LONDON         LHR NEW YORK        JFK BA    1 A 01JUL 1830 OK 2PC
... ...                ... ... ...          ... ..  ...  . ..... .... .. ...
... ...                ... ... ...          ... ..  ...  . ..... .... .. ...
FARE:USD 3991.00           FORM OF PAYMENT           CONDITIONS OF
TAXES/FEES/CHARGES:   CC VI4313******003709          CARRIAGE MAY BE
YC    5.00                                           INSPECTED ON
US  13.40    XT  84.07      E-TICKET NUMBER:          APPLICATION TO
TOTAL:USD 4093.47           125 240 9483299          BRITISH AIRWAYS
```

The Concorde Room at the Lounge Pavilion.

The main seating area inside the Concorde Room shortly before departure.

Alpha Golf (G-BOAG) at the gate. Today, she is preserved at the Museum of Flight, Seattle, United States.

was a definite air of excitement in the Concorde Room. Enthusiastic, camera-laden tourists mingled with seasoned business-people who just wanted to catch a few winks or get some work done on their laptops. I just stood at the window and stared at my ride of a lifetime.

The boarding announcement for BA 001 Concorde finally came. I took my seat 12D, grabbed my camera and told my seatmate I was going to get photos of the cabin. People were get-ting photos taken in their seats, in the aisles, and of the cabin speed displays showing 'Welcome to Concorde'. I looked at the small double-layered window. The inside window was about the size of a normal airliner window, but the outside one was only a bit larger than a passport.

The cradle seat seemed comfortable to sleep in fully reclined, but I didn't try it. The armrest was extremely narrow. When you folded it up, it twisted away into the seat … neat. As my seatmate pointed out, even though the seats were new, there were many clues we were in an aircraft from the 1970s. For example, on the overhead service units the reading lamp and the flight-attendant-call push buttons just looked old and yellowed. The audio adjustment knobs were rotary style.

Captain Andy Mills announced we would be taking off on Runway 27R and explained the noise abatement procedures ("to make us more neighbourly"). At 1 minute 16 seconds after brake release, engine power would be cut 90 percent and the angle of attack would be reduced. He explained this was perfectly normal and there was nothing to worry about. Then at 8,000 feet, we would go back to full power before reaching 26,000 feet for our subsonic cruise. Once over the ocean, we would go to full power with reheat [afterburners]. We took position on the runway and held for a while … the anticipation was killing me.

During our takeoff roll at 18:53, the engines sounded exactly as I'd heard when watching Concorde take off at New York JFK: like a fighter jet ... pure power. And loud, too! I sat up in my seat for a better look outside to see us speeding down the runway. Although I knew we were going fast, it wasn't really that noticeable unless I was looking at the things closer to the runway. We rotated and condensation appeared over the wing. Cool! The power was very quickly cut back and we pitched down significantly.

Shortly thereafter, cabin service started. The menu was passed out and the cabin staff went into overdrive, running around with our dinner service. One flight attendant served champagne while another served mineral water. Canapés followed. The captain came on and explained the reheats would be coming on again as we went through the transonic region. I thought this was the coolest part of the entire flight. The first pair of reheats came on, and I got a feeling of being pushed from behind. Then the next pair came on, got another kick from behind, and with it a feeling of acceleration. Within seconds, we are through the sound barrier and over Mach 1.

The ride was very smooth and there was no

Ben Wang poses next to the Mach meter at twice the speed of sound.

Appetizers: Lobster and tabbouleh salad.

Entrée: New season lamb cutlets with thyme and herb pancake wrapped in brioche, served with ginger and redcurrant compote.

Concorde touches down after an transatlantic flight. With her bullet speed, she could cross the Atlantic in less than half the time that her subsonic contemporaries could.
[© Adrian Meredith]

sonic boom to be heard in the cabin (but I already knew that). In fact, we went to Mach 1 so quickly that I had missed the exact moment because I was looking at the wrong side of the display – the side showing temperature and speed in miles per hour. When I saw cameras flashing I looked over to the other display and realized we were through the sound barrier. Now cold appetizers – lobster and tabbouleh salad – were served.

After reaching 42,000 feet at 19:25, I think the reheats went off at Mach 1.69, because I felt a bump. Another flight attendant took my order for the entrée. I chose the lamb. At 19:50, almost an hour after takeoff, we finally reached Mach 2. Everyone took a quick break from their meal and grabbed their cameras for photos of the speed displays. At 20:02, we were still climbing when we made our choice of cheese or dessert. I went with dessert – vanilla and white chocolate créme brulée, cassis compote and brandy snap – with a cup of tea. As the duty-free cart moved up the aisle, one man bought pretty much one or two of everything on offer, including the coveted 1976 Concorde limited edition Scotch whisky.

At 21:39 and at 57,000 feet, Captain Mills came on and explained we were beginning our deceleration and reaching our highest altitude. The curvature of the earth was not readily visible from one window. It was more apparent when I sat back and looked through both my windows using the bottom frame as a point of reference. However, it was very apparent across the aisle, through the windows on the opposite side.

The descent was very steep and we were quickly back down to Mach 1. Sometime after 22:00, the speed displays went off, replaced with, 'Thank you for flying Concorde'. At 22:18, the gears came down and we touched down four minutes later. Total flying time elapsed was 3 hours 29 minutes. The thrust reversers were very loud and there was a lot of braking motion. I had to grab my notepad and camera from the seat next to me so they wouldn't slide off. We made a short taxi to the gate at Terminal 7 where we arrived at 22:27 (local time in New York was 17:27).

I had left London at 18:30 and I was now in New York at 17:30. We had flown faster than the sun and I had gained an extra hour in my life! Later I asked Captain Mills what he was going to fly after Concorde. He responded dryly: "They want me to fly a 'bus'." We all chuckled. Another person asked: "Isn't that a bit of a downgrade?" The captain replied: "They should just put me out to grass, as I only have six months to go to retirement." Of course I did not forget to pick up my flight certificate.

The flight back home from New York to San José Airport, California, on a Boeing 757 was five and a half hours' long. Needless to say, it felt like an eternity.

A Guest in the Cockpit

"They say if you concentrate you can just feel a tiny lurch – matched in the cockpit by a blip on the instruments – as the aircraft punches its way through the sound barrier at Mach 1."

For most people a trip on Concorde was the epitome of luxury and speed. For those who never got the opportunity of flying on her, Paul Jeffries takes you through the supersonic adventure.

"Flying on Concorde was for most people who did so a once-in-a-lifetime thrill, an unforgettable experience, something that a few were privileged to do. Let's face it, the only other way to tear through the skies at twice the speed of sound was to become a fighter pilot - except you wouldn't be able to sup champagne as you relaxed in leather-bound luxury. I took my opportunity a few years back as a courier for British Airways World Cargo, carrying documents to New York in return for a Concorde ticket at a snip. For just £200 I would join hot-shot executives, celebrities and the generally well-heeled and fly British Airways' supersonic flagship to the Big Apple, returning by subsonic Boeing 747.

The supersonic transatlantic dash is a story told many times before, so I'd arranged to ride up front at the business end of Concorde flight BA003, squeezed into the tiny cockpit – this was before September 11, of course – with Captain Stuart Bates, First Officer Paul Randall and Senior Flight Engineer Alex Jones, to get a different view.

And what a view it was - at least, what I could see of it. Perched on the jump seat I was surrounded by a myriad of dials, switches, lights and levers that covered virtually every surface of the cockpit. I tried to make myself even smaller for fear of accidentally brushing against one of the controls and perhaps setting off alarm bells that would trigger my expulsion from the cockpit faster than an ejector seat.

Looking ahead, between Stuart and Paul as they ticked through the last of their pre-flight checks and fired up the feisty Olympus engines one by one, I could just see the taxiway in the grey distance before Concorde's drooped nose.

"Concorde is a lovely aircraft but it keeps you on your toes," Alex told me as he checked the plethora of instruments before him, throwing this switch and tweaking that knob, reminding me of an organ player - with several keyboards.

Most modern aircraft have computers to monitor the multitude of technical goings-on but Concorde's 1960s design meant everything was strictly manual. "Generally, it runs like clockwork," Alex added, "with the occasional exception."

Unfortunately, the occasional exception would be that evening when an overheat light for one of the four engines illuminated during taxiing. Within minutes of the aircraft returning to the stand, engineers were investigating the problem. "We have some of the most dedicated engineers on this aircraft," said Stuart after discussing the problem with licensed aircraft engineer Ian Fox. "I trust the guys on the ramp implicitly."

Ian worked with British Aerospace at Fairford in the 1960s and early 1970s during Concorde's development and knew the aircraft from nose cone to tailfin. He and his colleagues carried out a number of checks and decided that although the fault was minor, it would be safer - and quicker - to call the standby aircraft [a second Concorde ready to be used in case the scheduled one suffered technical problems]. Concorde G-BOAB took over her sister's duties.

I strapped myself into the jump seat and pulled on a set of headphones - my ticket into the strange world of air-traffic-control-and-flight-crew-tech talk. Sitting so far forward there was relatively little noise from the engines as Stuart and Paul hauled back on the throttles. But releasing the brakes was like letting go of a furious cat and we thundered down the runway at over 200 mph, eating up the tarmac at a dizzying rate, the terminal buildings and hotels either side disappearing into a bumpy blur. My stomach was in my mouth and then in my boots as we rocketed into the night sky, our passage no doubt viewed by people gazing up in awe - just as I had done - at the blue-orange glow of the reheats.

Climbing sharply, Concorde's drooping nose was raised and the aircraft's windscreen shield [visor] whirred upward and snapped into position. We were ready to go supersonic. The reheats were on, pumping gallons of fuel into the fiery exhaust nozzles on each engine, moon rocket-style, tearing the air with a roar like an Apollo space launch and thrusting us on towards the speed of sound. The instruments charting Concorde's increasing altitude and velocity (and plunging outside temperature) were mirrored in the cabin by displays on the bulkheads.

They say if you concentrated you could just feel a tiny lurch - matched in the cockpit by a blip on the instruments - as the aircraft punched its way through the sound barrier at Mach 1, around 675 mph. The afterburners stayed on until Concorde had reached between Mach 1.4 and 1.7; from there the speeds built slowly to Mach 2 - around 1,350 mph.

The higher the altitude, the thinner the air and the less resistance it produces; the colder the air, the more power is produced. Concorde flew at between 53,000 and 58,000 feet where the temperature could drop to minus 70°C. But there was a tight operational 'envelope', in which the best performance was obtained by optimizing altitude, air temperature and fuel burn rate.

Interestingly, it took 10.7 tonnes of fuel for Concorde to reach Mach 1.65 when the reheats were switched off - enough to carry a Boeing 757 well into Europe, explained Alex. Yet most of Concorde's passengers were sublimely unaware of such a feat of aviation engineering being played out, quite routinely, around them. Instead they were relaxing and soaking up the first-rate inflight service.

At the height of its career, Concorde's passengers would sip their way through some 1,800 cases of champagne each year, accompanied by heaps of caviar and smoked salmon. There was a lot of fine living to get done in a little over three hours - around half the time it took to fly to New York on a normal aircraft.

But it's not the luxury that made flying on Concorde so special. It was the technology that made it possible to carry a hundred passengers across the Atlantic faster than a jet fighter, it was the pilots who flew it and the engineers who looked after it. It was the thrill of experiencing one of civil aviation's greatest achievements, and it was the satisfaction of being able to say: "Yes, I flew on Concorde."

[© Adrian Meredith]

A Subsonic Experience

by Aris Pappas

With a mighty roar Concorde streaked down the runway, her reheats lit and first-class-plus passengers comfortably anticipating a short flight. The beautiful white livery on the airplane identified it as an Air France airliner, and it would eventually carry most of its passengers to Paris. But this May 1979 flight wasn't an Air France flight. It was Braniff International Flight 54, an early morning departure from Dallas, Texas to Dulles Airport, Washington DC. The flight and cabin crew were both Braniff, and Concorde was sporting a U.S. registration number, N94FD.

How did this come about? Enterprising executives at Braniff had noticed that the final flights of the day, by the British and French Concordes, were remaining overnight at Dulles because it was too late for a return trip to Europe and the planes needed to be in place for morning departures to London and Paris. But, there was enough time left in the day for a flight to Dallas, where Concorde could overnight, make an early departure, and be in place for the first morning flights across the Atlantic. An agreement was reached between the three airlines for either a French or a British Concorde to continue on to Texas every evening, with a fully qualified Braniff crew. Flight 54 was the Braniff flight that would return the aircraft to Dulles in time for its daily labors.

One problem had to be overcome: Federal Aviation Authority restrictions required U.S. airlines to fly only U.S.-registered aircraft. The solution was unique and a plane-spotter's dream … or nightmare. The French and British aircraft were formally reregistered to Braniff every evening at Dulles and then brought back to British and French registry every morning. This arrangement required a change in the outside registration on the aircraft, where a stick-on 'N' covered the 'G' or 'F' on the fuselage. Voila! F-94FD became N94FD.

The fares were quite reasonable for the short flight. According to The New York Times, the one-way fares to Paris and London were $1038 and $987 respectively. But the fare from Dallas to Dulles was only $169. It was that economical bargain that allowed me to upgrade an existing ticket on a scheduled 727 for the Concorde experience.

Braniff was trying to attract high-rolling business people headed to London or Paris, so they didn't skimp on the service. Concorde passengers had their own lounge at Dallas, where they could enjoy some pastries and, of course, champagne. At the appointed time we were taken out to the aircraft where I was a bit surprised at the relatively cramped conditions. Seating was four across in a cabin that while clean and neat, pretty much resembled the ubiquitous 727 and DC-9. Not uncomfortable, but not opulent either. First class on any Boeing 747 was significantly more impressive.

The captain welcomed us aboard and warned us that when the afterburners were closed during climb-out the sudden reduction in noise would make it sound like the engines had quit. He then told us that we would be flying higher and faster than other aircraft on the route, although with what sounded to me like regret, he also told us that we would not be flying faster than the speed of sound, thanks again to restrictions of the Federal Aviation Administration. We would, however, be flying roughly 100 mph faster than the Boeing 727s. In fact, our flight would be about half an hour less than the other jets on the route, whose regularly scheduled flight time was two and a half hours.

The meal service was exceptional. The air was smooth, but I found Concorde to feel a bit stiff. Perhaps the short delta wings did not flex a lot, but it was not enough to notice if you weren't an airplane fanatic trying to soak up every aspect of the experience. I'm not sure of our cruising altitude, but as promised we were able to watch as we passed 727s well below us. And, our cabin Mach meter got up to .97, just short of the speed of sound.

The only aspect of the entire flight that passengers were likely to notice, beside the roar at take-off, was the landing. Concorde's delta wing required an especially high angle of attack as the airplane slowed for landing. You definitely could tell that you were leaning way back in your seat because you had to look almost over your shoulder to see out the cabin window.

When we landed at Dulles, as expected, the crew welcomed us to Washington DC, thanked us for flying Braniff and wished everyone traveling on to Paris a good journey. To my embarrassment, I was the only passenger to get off at Dulles. So much for my sharing experiences with the high rollers!

Each Concorde had a total of hundred passenger seats in two cabins.

The cabin layout of Air France's Concordes during the 1970s.
[All photos © Aris Pappas]

Close-up of the cabin's overhead lights and the air ventilation system.

No matter if you flew at subsonic or supersonic speeds, Concorde's meal service was always exceptional.

Working as Cabin Crew on Concorde

"If I close my eyes I can still feel the thrust and noise of the engines as we hurtled down the runway and the realization that I had made my dreams come true to fly and be part of cabin crew on this historic aircraft."

– Suzanne O'Donoghue – Concorde cabin crew

For many flight attendants, or cabin crew, it was the ultimate experience and personal fulfilment to work on board Concorde and be part of such a special and loved aircraft. Many felt very privileged to even apply for one of the few positions available. Among these candidates was Suzanne O'Donoghue who had started her flying career with British Airways in October 1984 on long-haul Boeing 747 aircraft. It had been her life time ambition to fly on Concorde, so when she had the chance to work on her, she couldn't believe her luck:

"I decided to become a flight attendant for two reasons: I had just completed six months' backpacking around Australia and I definitely had the travel bug; the other was that my sister had just become a cabin crew member for British Airways. For years I had watched Concorde flying in and out of Heathrow and gazed in awe at her grace and beauty as she leapt into the sky with her burners glowing red. I eventually got my chance in 1995 when BA started to recruit for new cabin crew on board Concorde, I applied and went through the selection process with many other hopefuls. The process was quite intense, we had to sit formal interviews in front of a panel, write about why we should be selected, be immaculate in uniform and have an unblemished flying career with British Airways for longer than two years of service. I received my letter of acceptance and started my adventure flying on Concorde."

Suzanne remembers what it took to be a good cabin crew member: "You had to be quick! You needed to have a good sense of humour, and enjoy working in cramped, hot conditions. You had to be able to adapt, be friendly and of course you had to have a beaming smile at all times. The camaraderie between the crew members was lovely – it was like being part of an extended family where we all looked after each other, we all knew we were part of something very special."

Suzanne O'Donoghue was a Concorde crew member for three years.
[© Suzanne O'Donoghue]

A sign of Concorde pride – Suzanne's British Airways name badge.
[© Suzanne O'Donoghue]

Watch Video: Commercial Flight to New York

Please see instructions on page 2.

Working on board Concorde

"A typical day on Concorde would be checking into Compass Centre Crew check-in desk and going to the briefing room where you would meet the other crew on board the flight that day. We had six crew members on board, so it was always informal as we all generally knew each other. The Concorde uniform was the same as other fleets except the name badge; we also had to wear the uniform hat for boarding and disembarking. The in-charge crew member would inform all the crew of any important information that we needed to know, e.g. special passengers that we had or special meals on board. We would then choose our working positions for the flight. The flight deck usually joined us and gave us a flight time, weather report and ETA [estimated time of arrival] into our destination. Once we were all properly informed, paperwork signed and money collected for the duty-free sales, we would all climb onto the crew bus and be taken directly to the awaiting aircraft. As soon as we boarded we would check our safety equipment and the catering trolleys for the meals and canapés, all checks being given to the in-charge crew member; we would also make sure that drinks were served to the flight crew. We would make sure that the toilets and cabin had been properly 'dressed' so the seats and cabin looked immaculate for the passengers waiting in the lounge. Concorde passengers would have their coats taken from them in the Concorde lounge and it was the ground staff who brought the coats to the aircraft for us to safely stow them in the wardrobes before the passengers boarded. Even the suitcases were placed in zip-lock bags so that they wouldn't get dirty in the aircraft hold.

"We would then assume our boarding positions to welcome the passengers, and turn the music on as the passengers started to board. It was always known that certain passengers liked to sit in the front three rows of the aircraft. The front cabin seated forty passengers and the rear cabin sixty, both cabins receiving the same service. When boarded all the passengers would be offered vintage champagne or soft drinks, hot towels, menus and newspapers. We would then take a drinks order to be served straight after take-off. Then it would be push back and the safety briefing where you would feel the excited anticipation as Concorde prepared for lift-off.

"We were airborne within thirty seconds, it felt like taking off in a space rocket. Once airborne we would start the drinks round served on silver trays followed by canapés of caviar with mother-of-pearl spoons.

"After a second round of drinks we would start to lay up for the meal service with

Throughout Concorde's career her service and food met the highest standards, adding to the exclusivity of a Concorde flight. *[© Adrian Meredith]*

tablecloths and fine china, linen and napkins with buttonholes in. Usually the cold starter would be seafood, followed by a choice of main: fillet of prime beef or game. Salad was also always offered. Then it would be the cheese selection served with vintage port. Dessert would be a fresh fruit salad. After this we would serve tea and coffee with petit fours and mints. The wine list was all vintage. I remember one of our longer-serving crew members saying that he wanted to come back as a Concorde sink when he died, as we had to pour any open bottles of wine and champagne down the sink before landing. We also offered cigars in the days of onboard smoking.

"Once completed we would offer duty frees. Before landing the crew would hand out Concorde gifts to the passengers which could be silver hip flasks, bottle openers, address books, photo albums etc. All of this would have to be completed in under three and a half hours which was sometimes a challenge if you had a full aircraft of hundred passengers."

Flight attendants posing with their beloved Concorde. She was not just a work place, she was a place of dreams. *[© British Airways]*

"The smile and enthusiasm of our passengers as they disembarked after landing was always a real reward for us."

– Annick Moyal, Air France Concorde cabin crew

Annick Moyal joined Air France in 1973. Five years on, while working as a flight attendant on long-haul flights to East Africa and the Indian Ocean, her supervisor asked her to join Concorde: "My training started in 1978 as Air France needed additional flight attendants for the newly established route to New York. An exact cabin mock-up was our 'classroom' for two weeks. In a few words, we learned how to move the trolleys and serve our passengers in such a narrow working space. Our training motto was 'l'Excellence à la Française'." Annick describes her working day on board: "After our briefing we would check the passenger list to be aware of our 'guests' of the day. For security reasons, some of them – businessmen, bankers, politicians – had checked in under assumed names. The list also provided information about various passenger requests such as special menus or certain passengers' habits we should be aware of. We would meet our regular and new passengers in the lounge which was a nice way to greet them.

"After take-off we would start our service by offering our passengers a glass of champagne and caviar toast points. Then lunch or dinner would follow, which for example could be paté foie gras, lobster or caviar. Our passengers were offered special menus by well-known French chefs, prepared on the ground by the Air France catering department dedicated to our Concorde clients. We only had to warm them up in the galley ovens. Vegetarian, Indian, kosher, or Muslim dishes were available and served upon request. After the meal, we would offer various French cheeses. Concorde carried France's best products including marvellous Bordeaux and Burgundy wines. Before the tragic events of 9/11 security standards were different, so our passengers were allowed to visit the flight deck.

"As soon as the descent began we handed out customs forms and addressed various individual passenger requests such as finding a helicopter to get from JFK Airport to Manhattan or chartering a private aircraft. Before touching down in New York, we would secure the cabin and as soon as we had landed, we returned the coats we had collected before the flight. The smiles and enthusiasm of our passengers as they

Flight attendants on the Air France Concordes could choose between different uniform colours. The first uniform (1976–85) was designed by Patou, the second (1986–94) and the third (1994–2003) by Nina Ricci. This photo shows the second uniform.
[© Air France Museum]

From the mid-1990s to Concorde's retirement in 2003, male Air France flight attendants wore spencer jackets while serving meals.
[© Air France Museum]

disembarked after landing were always a real reward for us. Concorde helped me get together with my husband Claude. I was introduced to him during a dinner party at a New York restaurant, and I met him again as a passenger on Concorde two years later."

Claude Moyal remembers his flights: "Although I wasn't one of Concorde's most important passengers, I certainly was one of the most frequent flyers, with about 200 flights. My professional career had been closely connected to the Anglo-Saxon business community: I used to work in the reinsurance sector which is widely unknown to the general public as the business negotiations take place between insurance professionals and their reinsurance counterparts – the reinsurance experts are the financial backers of insurance companies. During the later phase of my career, I worked with the American group 'The Green Stamps Company' (Sperry Hutchinson), in charge of one of its subsidiaries. With reinsurance being an international business I had American and European clients and had to travel across the world to various financial markets: I had two offices in the United States (New York and Los Angeles), and two in Europe (Paris and London). To stay a step ahead of my competitors I used to take Concorde to New York where my head office was located. After a few days of working there I would go on a regular (subsonic) flight to Los Angeles. When flying with American airlines, their captains would always inform us passengers that there was a Concorde taking off for everyone to see as she seemed to enjoy the privilege of being allowed to depart before all other commercial flights. Being a Frenchman, one

The last cabin design of the Air France Concordes was created by French designer André Putman in the mid-1990s. Putman, who flew with Concorde several times, also designed the seats and the cutlery.
[© Air France Museum]

Annick Moyal with her husband Claude. She worked as a Concorde flight attendant from 1978 until 1989.
[© Annick Moyal]

can imagine how proud I was listing to the captain's enthusiastic praise about Concorde... I felt as if I had built that aircraft! I would stop by at my Paris office at 8:30, arrive at CDG Airport for departure at 11:00 and touch down at JFK at 9:00 local time (15:00 Paris time). There, I would work until 16:00 (22:00 Paris time) and then go to my apartment where I would call my L.A. office. Being on two continents on the same day was a privilege only Concorde could offer.

"But by the end of the day, I would drop dead in my bed! Although my body would wake me up in the middle of the night at 3:00 New York time, this at least would give me the opportunity to make my mandatory phone calls to my Paris office at 9:00 Paris time. This was a time when video conferencing was not common yet. My intercontinental travellings lasted approximately twelve years, until 1987. The following year I got married to Annick."

A Supersonic Challenge

"She was complex and full of surprises. Sometimes the fleet would be as good as gold, other times all five would play up. I sometimes wondered if they talked to each other!"

Flight Engineers

At one time there were hundreds of them at Air France and British Airways. But with the march of technology, the number of flight engineers on board commercial aircraft dwindled until they were only needed on Concorde. There are a number of candidates for the title 'Unsung Aviation Hero'. Although the list of potential recipients is long, one group of people frequently made an appearance at the top: flight engineers - or engineering officers to give them their correct titles. They have been an integral part of both Air France and British Airways since the flying boat days of the 1930s. Concorde's retirement in 2003 witnessed more than just the end of commercial supersonic travel. She was the last jet at Air France and British Airways with flight engineers working in the cockpit, so her retirement also marked the end of that role within both airlines. At their peak in the 1980s, Air France and British Airways each had numerous flight engineers.

Their working day started about an hour before take-off, when they would carry out a strictly organized routine of inspections and pre-flight checks. Once airborne, the flight engineer's work continued, constantly monitoring the aircraft's fuel, hydraulics, electrical systems and engines. This also combined the integrated duties of flight path monitoring and navigation, work they shared with the pilots.

Warren Hazelby spent ten years years as British Airways' chief flight engineer: "The three-man crew concept was introduced in the early 1970s and required the flight engineers to be trained on basic navigation, weather and aircraft performance. Pilots were given more in-depth technical knowledge and three crew members worked as a team with the captain in charge. It was a great success and made the flight engineer a key member of the team." Ian Kirby remembers, why he decid-

The flight engineer was a key member of the flight crew until computers gradually took over.
[© Air France Museum]

ed to become a Concorde flight engineer: "I am an engineer at heart and to just be the pilot of such a machine was not enough for me. I had to know and understand Concorde's workings, how she achieved her aims and what to do when she refused to cooperate from time to time."

Concorde was the supreme example of the flight engineer's art, with four times as many controls as the classic Boeing 747. Pierre Grange who was an Air France 747 pilot and who would become a Concorde pilot in 1984, remembers his first visit to a Concorde in Mexico: "I put my hand on the control panels and the throttles and said to myself that it would be amazing to be able to fly this machine. While standing in front of the flight engineer's panel, I immediately understood that the work of the flight engineer must be very complex." Former Air France Concorde ground engineer Patrick Sevestre agrees: "It is the number of fuel system gauges and switches that is most impressive. You have to find your way around." Pierre Grange: "A Concorde flight crew is crew of three with each of them performing a specific task as part of the cooperation with the two other flight crew members. Therefore, we always had to be attentive and anticipate what may happen next."

The flight engineer's role also involved controlling

Former Concorde flight engineer Ian Kirby in the pilot seat.
[© Ian Kirby]

the position of the centre of gravity by moving fuel fore and aft during flight. "That was the ultimate in team work," Warren Hazelby says. "The movement of the fuel and acceleration/deceleration must be performed in unison to maintain adequate flight control."

The demise of the flight engineer was pretty well inevitable as the jet age slowly but surely ushered in a change from five-person flight crews to two. Many of the flight engineer's tasks are now performed by computer. The advent of the 747-400 in the 1980s signalled the beginning of the end when Boeing removed the flight engineer panel and systems became computerized.

Gérard Duval began his

aviation career as an Air France flight engineer on the Caravelle and various Airbus airliners. While working as an instructor training foreign flight crews on the Airbus A300 at the Airbus facility in Toulouse, this period in the early 1980s was decisive for him: "While the Airbus A310 was undergoing a two-person flight crew certification, several flight test engineers had begun their conversion courses into professional pilots. I took advantage of my time in Toulouse to take the theory exams for the airline pilot qualification and improve my flying skills on light aircraft (I had held private pilot licence since 1973). Toulouse was also an opportunity to discover the world of flight tests and to meet former French

Concorde test pilots Jean Pinet, Gilbert Defer, Henri Perrier, and Jean-Pierre Flamand as well as Alan Heywood and Peter Holding from the British Aircraft Corporation. When I returned to Air France, my conversion to an airline pilot had to wait a while as I was appointed to the technical flight operations department where I wrote and translated the Airbus A310 operating manual. Eventually, I became a Concorde pilot in 1999 and flew her until 2003." It is estimated that in 1980 more than 3,000 aircraft carried flight engineers all over the world as part of the crew. Concorde was the last jet to have them flying in the cockpit alongside the pilots. Today they are virtually gone.

Two Air France Concordes inside their maintenance hangar. [© Jean-Philippe Lemaire]

Ground Engineers

Most people who have worked on Concorde talk about their special relationship with the aircraft, but perhaps none knew her quite so well as the French and British engineers who knew her - quite literally - inside out. Concorde engineers had to work in tight spaces, sometimes using mirrors to see the parts they were working on. And unlike modern aircraft like the Boeing 777, there was no plug-in self-diagnostic equipment to locate a problem - the engineers had to track it down themselves, using knowledge and experience accumulated over many years. "We cursed her every day for her complexity," says British Airways senior technician Robin Chatterjee who can't stifle his affection for long. "Even after all that time, I couldn't stop admiring her when she came

in to land or took off." And the challenges of working with supersonic technology had been there from the start, going back to the pioneering days of André Turcat and Brian Trubshaw. Karl Howard-Norris agrees that she was a challenging aircraft. "She was complex and full of surprises. Sometimes the fleet would be as good as gold, other times all five (of originally seven Concordes) would play up. I sometimes wondered if they talked to each other!"

Overseas engineer Miles Jordan maintained the aircraft at some of the exotic destinations she flew to including Rome, Cairo and Nairobi, where she was swamped by a sea of people on her first visit there. The weather often posed an additional challenge. He remembers changing a hydraulic pump in Bahrain where he had to deal

with a hot engine in ambient temperatures of 44° centigrade. "You ended up blowing on your hands to keep them cool to undo the nuts and bolts," he said. But he would not have missed it for the world. "I have worked on Concorde from the build, right through her life, and I think she is a wonderful aircraft."

Patrick Sevestre started his career at the Air France training centre for aircraft mechanics at the age of fifteen. After working on the Sud Aviation Caravelle as well as on Boeing and Airbus airliners, Patrick eventually maintained the French Concordes as a ground engineer in equally exotic places, such as the Senegalese capital Dakar which served as a stopover for the Rio de Janeiro flights. Today, Patrick is a member of a team of dedicated volunteers caring for

the two Concordes on display at the Musée de l'air et de l'espace at Le Bourget near Paris, one being the prototype 001 and the other the Air France production aircraft Sierra Delta. Asked what in his opinion makes a good ground engineer, he answers: "Generally speaking, it is the knowledge of the aircraft's systems and the associated record-keeping. More specifically, it is an awareness of various problems and the response thereof in the analytical processes and the ability to maintain a balanced perspective.

Former British Airways ground engineer Ricky Bastin summarizes a typical working day: "Concorde would be rolled out of the hangar following her regular post-flight maintenance. The aircraft would then be towed from the engineering area where she would be

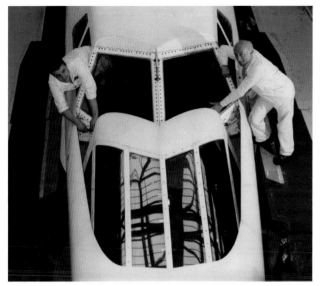

Many of Concorde's design features, such as the droop nose and sliding windscreen (visor), presented engineers with unique maintenance tasks.
[© Adrian Meredith]

Concorde ground engineer (BA) Carl Percy uses a bore-scope to carry out an internal inspection of one of the engines.
[© Adrian Meredith]

Patrick Sevestre as a Concorde ground engineer in Dakar, 1982.
[© Patrick Sevestre]

prepared for flight. The aircraft would be refuelled, the cabin 'prepped' for service by cleaning staff and the catering would be loaded into the forward and rear galleys. While all this was going on, ground engineers would carry out a thorough check of the aircraft's various systems, to get early warning of any issues that would need to be addressed before flight. One hour before departure the flight and cabin crews arrive to prepare the aircraft and cabin for flight. For my own description, I'd look at the defects that were outstanding from the previous night, ensure that there were resources in place to address these, and make sure that the service aircraft were serviceable. Once the aircraft had been towed from the airline's engineering base I would travel to the terminal with my team, and on arrival carry out the systems checks before the crew arrived, handing the aircraft over to them. Between now and departure my team and I would wait in 'Concorde Tech', and listen out for any problems on VHF radio."

Patrick Sevestre describes what he and his team at Air France had to do after Concorde's landing:

"As soon as the aircraft had arrived at the parking space, it had to be 're-sponsive' for the technical debrief. Therefore, we met with the flight crew to go through their notes taken during the flight and discuss technical problems that might have occurred. Each note had to be addressed and each problem had to be completely taken care of before the next flight which meant that we sometimes were busy working on the aircraft for many hours."

Although Concorde was a very demanding aircraft, British Airways fleet planning engineer Chris Had-jigeorgiou stresses that it is important to celebrate all the good things about her: "We probably won't see another supersonic aircraft for two or three generations. People love this white bird - but we needn't be too sad."

CONCORDE
AS AN ICON

"... unrivalled to this day for her technical performance and aesthetics, Concorde will remain a pilot's grail for eternity."

— Béatrice Vialle, former AF Concorde co-pilot

Concorde speeds down the runway for take-off – a moment charged with excitement.
[© British Airways]

Sleek and slim, Concorde was unlike anything anyone had ever seen before. She captured the public's imagination for her looks as much as for her speed. The design teams' quest for the perfect aerodynamic shape also led to a beautiful and timeless birdlike look that remains as eye-catching and elegant today as it was when it was rolled out in 1967. It is testament for Concorde's iconic reputation that she served as the flagship for Air France and British Airways for more than a quarter of a century. When people talk about

Concorde rotates and condensation appears over her delta wing.
[© British Airways]

her, they describe her the way one might describe an international superstar: graceful, glamorous, classic – peppered with 'oohs' and 'ahhs'. The love affair with Concorde echoed through the words of pilots, cabin crew members, engineers, staff, passengers, and anyone who touched or was touched by this supersonic icon in some way.

"As some of the Concorde pilots loved to say: 'There are fewer Concorde pilots in the world than there are astronauts!'"

– Iona Ferguson, former BA Concorde flight attendant

To see the curvature of the earth for the first time is something you never forget."

– Suzanne O'Donoghue, former BA Concorde flight attendant

Concorde's fuselage stretched about ten inches in supersonic flight. She was built with a flexible structure for ultimate strength. After more than 5,000 hours of test and endurance flying, Concorde was the most thoroughly proven airliner ever to go into service. The French affectionately called Concorde the 'Bel Oiseau' – the beautiful bird.
[© Air France Museum]

To commemorate Concorde's 20th anniversary in 1989, the French-built production test aircraft Sierra Bravo (F-WTSB) received a glittering blue, red and paintwork. *[© Air France Museum]*

*"The only supersonic aircraft in operation, the captains
of all the other airlines on the ground would tell
their passengers: 'look left [or right] – Concorde!'"*

– Frank Debouck, former AF Concorde manager

Six Concordes celebrate Ten-Year Anniversary
Photographer Adrian Meredith remembers taking this remarkable photograph on Boxing Day (26 December) 1985 at London Heathrow: "This shoot was set up as a fall-back option, in case the air-to-air photography undertaken on Christmas Eve 1985[see pages 128-133] wasn't sufficient. We arranged for six out of the seven British Airways Concordes to be towed into a tight fan formation which took the ground engineers six hours to complete. We demonstrated the formation with small Concorde models beforehand to show to the engineers the placements. A helicopter had been hired for the air-to-ground shoot. I was strapped into a safety harness, hanging out of the side of the helicopter. The conditions were so precarious that Captain Brian Walpole insisted we could not shoot directly overhead of the six Concordes because, if we crashed, we would have wiped out the entire BA Concorde fleet. The helicopter pilot finally agreed to take me up for just ten minutes and I shot from the side, to capture this photograph."
[© Adrian Meredith]

Escorted by French Air Force Mirage F1 fighters, Concorde Sierra Delta (F-BTSD), under the command of Captain Raymond Machavoine, takes President François Mitterrand to Djibouti in the Horn of Africa for a state visit, on 12 December 1987. When Mitterrand (inset photo) decided to fly to French Guyana (via Dakar) to attend an Ariane rocket launch, he requisitioned two Air France Concordes – one for the actual flight fitted out with a presidential suite, and one as a stand-by (back-up) aircraft at Charles de Gaulle Airport.
[© Armée de l'Air Française / Inset photo: U.S. Dept. of Defense]

Alpha Charlie (G-BOAC) was considered the flagship of British Airways as her registration featured the initials of BOAC (British Overseas Airways Corporation), the predecessor of British Airways
[© John Powell / johnnypowell.net]

"... I was impressed with the shape and construction and the general feeling of looking at the future."

– Philip Cairns, former BA Concorde ground engineer

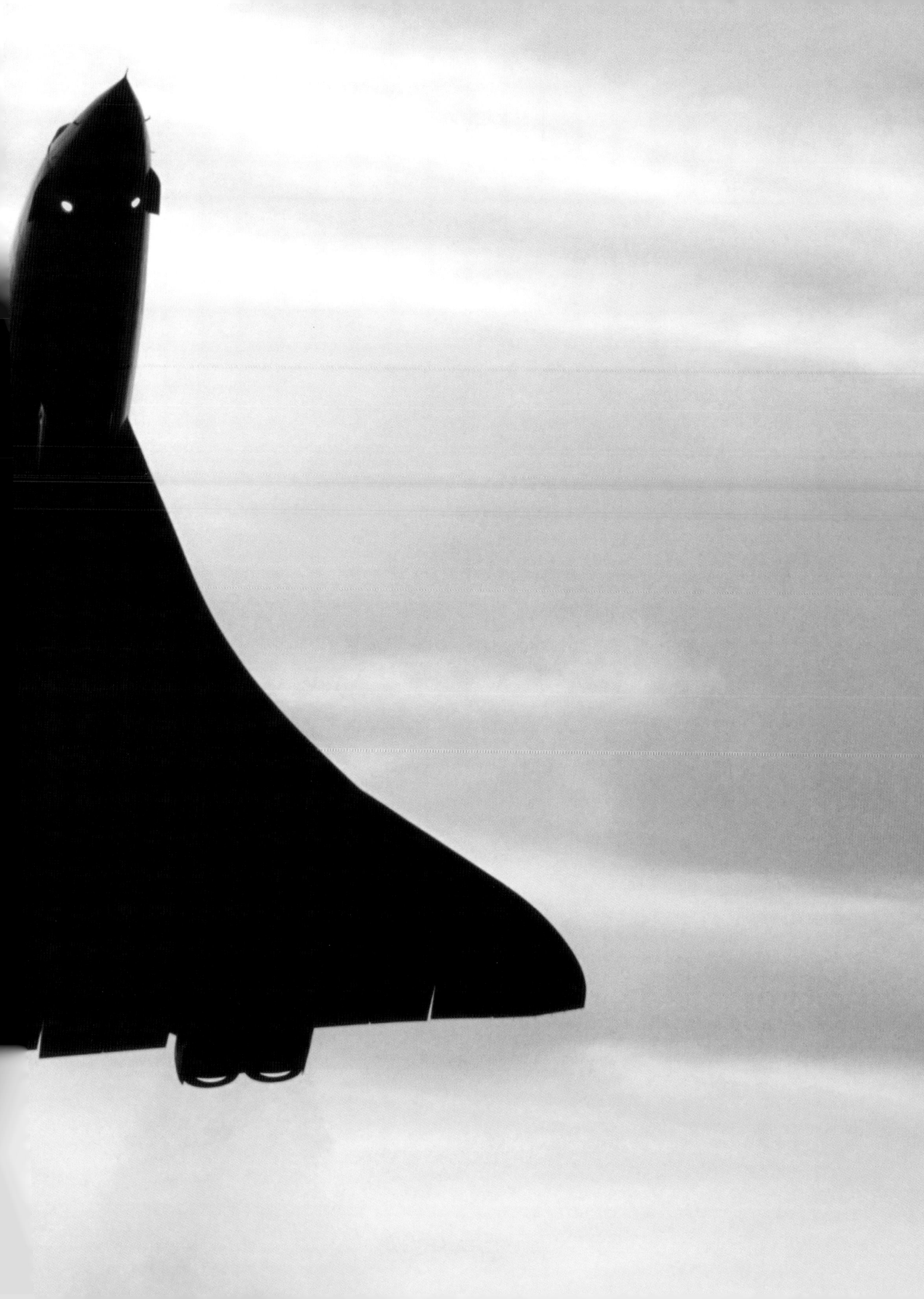

[© John Powell / johnnypowell.net]

Imaging an Icon

by Adrian Meredith

Adrian Meredith – pictured here with his wife Angela – has been a commercial and aviation photographer since the 1970s. He has won numerous photography awards including the 'Ilford Photographer of The Year 1976'. For many years, Adrian undertook assignments with some of the world's leading airlines including British Airways, Emirates, Qatar and Virgin Airlines.

ty seconds in succession, something that had never been done before.

Being December, the weather was dark and gloomy, the sun low and watery. We rose above the clouds, to brighter skies where we circled and, as we looked down, we saw each Concorde pop through the clouds like a bullet. After the fourth aircraft emerged we quickly descended and gave chase at full throttle

to try and catch them up. They started to manoeuvre and steadily flew into position for the first formation – 'Diamond', then 'Echelon' and then 'Swan'.

The weather was very poor, and each time the Concordes set up for a different formation, a bank of cloud would roll in, and the four aircraft would have to break off their positioning for safety reasons. This gave me a brief opportu-

During Concorde's twenty-seven years of service I have had the privilege of shooting many dramatic shots of her. One day I was asked by British Airways to shoot the famous four Concordes in formation to promote and commemorate the tenth anniversary of Concorde's commercial service. This was one of the most important and exciting photographic assignments I have ever undertaken, and very prestigious for Concorde. The date was Christmas Eve, 24 December 1985, the only day possible to photograph four of the Concordes together, as they were not flying commercially.

Many hours were spent at the briefing sessions, to ensure the formations were tidy to military precision. Different formations were discussed

and the pilots finally decided upon the 'Diamond', the 'Echelon' and the 'Swan'. Nothing like this had ever been commercially done before. Concorde senior captains Brian Walpole and John Cook were experienced pilots and had a wealth of experience of formation flying from their days in the Royal Air Force. My task was to capture in essence the group formations. The flight plan was to take off from Heathrow, fly to Filton in Bristol, the home of Concorde, down the Bristol Channel, and return to London.

The Lear Jet I'd be flying in had to be fitted with optically corrective glass in the windows that wouldn't distort the camera's image. We were to take off first. Special permission had to be granted for each Concorde to take off every thir-

HM Queen Elizabeth II on board Concorde in 1977. The Royal Family were frequent travellers on Concorde.
[© Adrian Meredith]

The late Queen Mother enjoys a visit to Concorde's flight deck on her eighty-fifth birthday in 1985.
[© Adrian Meredith]

The Queen waves as Concorde salutes the Royal Yacht *Britannia* off Barbados, 1977.
[© Adrian Meredith]

nity to liaise with the pilots between shooting. As soon as the Concordes were back in another formation, I knew the photography would have to be quick and sharp. On one occasion we banked steeply, sweeping over the top of the formation to get perfect overhead shots. Other photography was taken side on. During one stage of a particular formation, the Concordes' wingtips were only seventy feet from each other. The entire exercise took an hour and 45 minutes, and all four aircraft returned safely home, and thankfully I had all the shots in the can.

Throughout my years, I have encountered many air-to-air shoots on a variety of different aircraft, but Concorde was something special. She is a very photogenic icon, a photographer's dream, and is still everyone's favourite aircraft. She could look totally different from various angles: take-offs and landings can look fantastic if shot with a long telephoto lens, her shape resembling a sweeping eagle or a descending swan negotiating a landing position. The most enjoyable part of capturing images of Concorde was when we covered the air-to-air assignments. Some wonderful photographs were made possible with the use and assistance of the famous Red Arrows, and also an RAF Tornado flying alongside Concorde whilst executing various manoeuvres. Moreover, I had the honour and privilege of covering numerous Royal assignments – with The Queen, Prince Philip, Prince Charles and Princess Diana. I also covered The Queen Mother's special Concorde flight to celebrate her eighty-fifth birthday.

Adrian Meredith – pictured here with his wife Angela – has been a commercial and aviation photographer since the 1970s. He was won numerous awards including the 'Ilford Photographer of The Year 1976'. For many years, Adrian has undertaken assignments with some of the world's leading airlines including British Airways, Emirates, Qatar and Virgin.

Princess Diana waves to the photographers while boarding Concorde.
[© Adrian Meredith]

The four aircraft in swan-like 'Concorde' formation over Land's End, Cornwall.

The four Concordes line up in 'echelon starboard' formation.

Concorde's Display Flights

by Ian Dick

Ian Dick, former commander of the Red Arrows.
[© Ian Dick]

Besides their service as exclusive passenger airliners, both France and Great Britain utilized their Concordes for aerial displays as symbols of national pride. These memorable flights took place with each country's premier aerobatic display team, the Patrouille de France of the French Air Force and the Red Arrows of the British Royal Air Force. Representing speed, dynamics, and precision, each is the public face of its national air force.

Between 1973 and 2002, Concorde flew with the Patrouille de France and the Red Arrows on various occasions including the French National Day parade on 14 July in Paris and Queen Elizabeth's Golden Jubilee in 2002. These spectacular displays, watched by thousands of people, were captured in beautiful photographs. Ian Dick, a former commander of the Red Arrows, describes how the first-ever formation photo of Concorde and an aerobatic display team was made possible:

"I remember the day that the late Arthur Gibson – one of the best aviation photographers during the 1970s – called me and said: "Ian, I think it's time we got a photo of the Team in formation with Concorde … before the French beat us to it." I was excited because here was the opportunity to get the publicity photo we'd been waiting for, and British Aerospace owed us a favour. When the company's flight-test team wanted air-to-air footage taken of the pro-

totype Concorde during her approaches to land, they chose Arthur Gibson as the photographer; the late Ted Girdler – one of the Team's pilots – flew him in a Folland Gnat. It was a successful partnership, and the company were delighted with the results.

I knew John Cochrane – the Deputy Chief Test Pilot – well enough to feel comfortable ringing him. He was not surprised by my call. I sensed he knew that it was 'payback' time. He discussed it with Brian Trubshaw – the Chief Test Pilot – who happily agreed, but with one proviso: it had to be done at the end of a test flight as Concorde flew back to Fairford. Nothing could interfere with their test schedule or flights, and there could be no special arrangements. It was a one-off.

It was not very difficult to arrange because the team was based at nearby Kem-

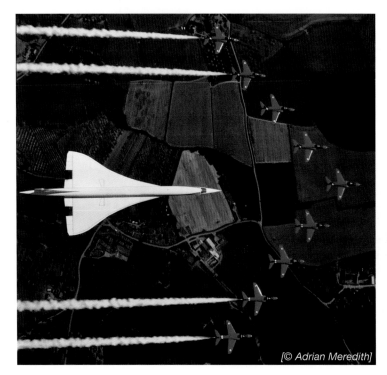

[© Adrian Meredith]

British pride: Concorde flying in formation with the Red Arrows. *[Photo by Arthur Gibson/© Adrian Meredith]*

Concorde and the Red Arrows overfly the North Sea as a rehearsal for the Queen's Jubilee Flypast, 2002.
[© MoD]

ble. We would get a call from air traffic control when Concorde was on her way home, get airborne and loiter just north of Kemble as Concorde made her approach to Fairford. Our paths would cross!

It was late when we got the call to get airborne, after 4 p.m. on a dismal day in April. The Gnat did not have a lot of fuel, and we had to orbit for longer than I had anticipated. I was getting a bit anxious about our fuel state when John came up on frequency, and we were able to finesse the join-up. At the appropriate moment, I set the Team up on an easterly heading at 1,000 feet in 'Big Nine' formation. The Team manager was ready in his Gnat with Arthur in the rear seat. I couldn't see what was happening, but I heard John's Scottish accent announce that he was "All aboard". The Manager called, "Smoke on go" and did a wide, sweeping barrel roll over the whole formation – first one way and then back the other way. Arthur had only two opportunities to 'get it in the can'. He did not let us down.

It was only afterwards, when we were having a drink in the bar with John, that we learnt they had been on a supersonic test flight over the Bay of Biscay flying Concorde at over 1,000 mph. This meant that they were wearing bulky pressure flying suits and special helmets akin to the ones worn by astronauts. Not the ideal headgear for flying a supersonic aircraft in close formation with the Red Arrows! John did a marvellous job and, as he flew Concorde in behind us, he heard Brian exclaim, "Bloody hell, I didn't know you were going to fly this close!"

Concorde Fox Alpha (F-BVFA) during her flypast with the Patrouille de France at the La Ferté-Alais Air Show in northern France, 1987.
[© Bernard Charles / art-avia.eu]

"Concorde is part of France's heritage, to be mentioned in the same breath as the Eiffel Tower, the Notre Dame cathedral, and the luxury liner SS France."

– Alain Verschuere, former AF Concorde purser

Capturing Concorde in photographs has always been a delight for professionals and enthusiasts alike. French photographer Bernard Charles recalls taking a memorable photo of Air France's Fox Alpha (F-BVFA) on 7 June 1987:

"I used to visit the La Ferté-Alais Air Show for several years but that year was special as Concorde was scheduled to make a flypast with the Patrouille de France. Over the years I had repeatedly watched the white bird taking off and landing at Charles de Gaulle Airport where spectators could only stand quite far away from the runways. At La Ferté, however, until 1989, the crowd was allowed to watch the air show from a much closer vantage point. I remember that as Concorde approached, I felt the vibrations generated by her engines rising up from the ground through my entire body, in particular when the reheats kicked in for the 'go around'! This was a unique experience; it is worth mentioning that these flypasts took place with a hundred passengers on board.

"I had two more opportunities to relive the experience that year: at Le Bourget during the Paris Air Show in June and at the Lognes Air Show [east of Paris] in September 1987. During both these shows I decided to walk to the runway threshold to stand exactly below Concorde's flight path, thus feeling the engines' heat and thrust while wearing ear protection. As far as I can remember the only aircraft that has given me a similar thrill was the Rockwell B-1B Lancer which I had seen at Le Bourget as well. This was not surprising as the Lancer is almost in the same category as Concorde in terms of power and thrust."

SS *France*

The SS *France* was a grand transatlantic liner, built in the tradition of the SS *Normandie*, as an oceangoing showcase for France. Commissioned in 1962 and operated by the Compagnie Générale Transatlantique (French Line), the 1,037-feet (316m) vessel was the longest passenger ship ever built until the launching of the *Queen Mary 2* in 2004. Due to the 1973 oil crisis and the increasing oil price the ship's already-high operating costs rose further, thus prompting the French government to subsidize the then in-development Concorde. Without government support the SS *France* could no longer operate. In 1974 she was withdrawn from service and eventually

The SS *France* was a maritime symbol of French design, engineering and prestige. She was later sold to Norwegian Cruise Line and renamed *Norway*. She was scrapped in 2008.
[© Jon Archibald]

sold to Norwegian Cruise Line. If she had still been in service when Concorde commenced her commercial flights in 1976, it would have been possible for transatlantic travellers to sail to New York on board the SS *France* and fly back to Paris on Air France's

Concorde as both could offer a combination of the most exclusive means of crossing the Atlantic. To this day, both the SS *France* and the Air France Concordes are icons of France as are the British Airways Concordes and the (retired) liner *Queen Elizabeth 2 (QE2)*.

An Air France Concorde in formation with the Alpha Jets of the Patrouille de France.
[© Dre Peijmen]

In Formation with the Queen Elizabeth 2

"… that is the picture of the century."

— Captain John Hutchinson in
Mach 2 magazine, August 2018

Richard Thomas, team leader of the Red Arrows from 1984 to 1987 recalls, how one of Concorde's most iconic photos came into being: "Somewhere about late spring of 1984, someone had the bright idea that a photograph of the Red Arrows in formation with Concorde over the QE2 [*Queen Elizabeth 2*] would make history. Planning for the sortie took the best part of a year and involved any number of agencies. Getting the three participants in the same place at the same time would not be easy as all had busy schedules. However, the date was fixed for 18 May 1985. The final briefing complete, the Team positioned at RAF Lyneham in southern England in readiness for the actual sortie. The weather was not perfect but acceptable. After take-off we headed for the south coast around Weymouth. We expected to join up with Concorde as we coasted out into the English Channel and exactly as planned she appeared below and out to our port side. The sight of Concorde was a great thrill and meant that the first part of the sortie had worked – I felt greatly relieved but only for a moment as the next and most difficult part of the trip was coming up: finding QE2. However, in the meantime and unbeknown to most of the Team, the Concorde crew were having difficulties with the Royal Navy controller as they had been told that the airspace was closed and that the aircraft would not be allowed into the ranges. The crew explained quickly that this was a special flight that taken a year to arrange and had been approved by a whole raft of agencies including the Royal Navy. The controller would not give way. However, after a short break while both sides thought about their next move, the controller came back with a proposed solution: the aircraft carrier HMS *Illustrious*, which was working up in the ranges, had a families' day and if Concorde overflew the ship after the QE2 flypast she might be allowed into the controlled airspace. The Concorde crew instantly agreed while thinking how to get their own back on the Navy! Without GPS or any other help apart from Concorde's navigation system, QE2 appeared just as planned near the Isle of Weight on her way into Southampton. The photographer for the mission was the legendary Arthur Gibson, who had been working with the Team since it was formed twenty years before. To get the picture Arthur wanted, overflight height and distance out from the ship caused much discussion. The calculations proved correct and the result was an iconic picture that encapsulated the 'Best of British'. What a relief!"

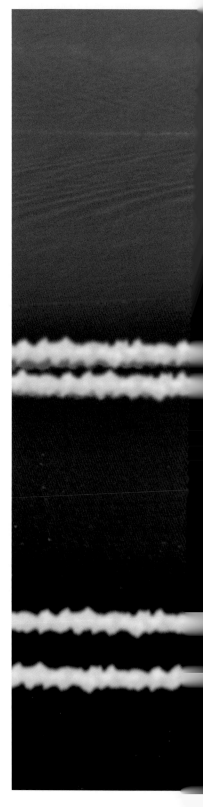

The 'Best of British' – the *QE2* with Concorde and the Red Arrows. The pilot had to fly upside down so that Arthur Gibson could get this shot. The *QE2* was operated by Cunard as both a transatlantic liner and a cruise ship from 1969 to 2008. Today, she is a floating hotel in Dubai.
[Photo by Arthur Gibson / © Adrian Meredith]

Supersonic Star Gazing

"Sir Paul McCartney liked ... to start strumming some of his favourite songs in mid-air at supersonic speeds."

The exclusivity of supersonic travel meant that when you flew Concorde you joined an elite and illustrious band of travellers. Over the years she carried world leaders and celebrities, as well as the fabulously wealthy. For all of them aviation's grandest aircraft was a magnet. Concorde was the last word in glamour, the choice of royalty, the aristocracy, rock stars, movie stars and top businessmen. And, from impromptu songs by former Beatles to record-breaking golf stunts, anything could happen aboard. If there is one thing they always seemed to agree upon, it was that the beautiful big bird was simply the only way to cross the Atlantic – in comfort, style and speed. The medium became the message: to travel supersonically, to flash between time zones and land before you had taken off, mattered more than where you were going.

The Celebrity Choice

To fly Concorde was to add your name to passenger lists oozing glamour and wealth. On the same seats might have reposed the bottoms of Sean Connery, Catherine Deneuve, Bridget Bardot, Henry Kissinger, Robert Redford, Jack Nicholson, Jeanne Moreau, Mick Jagger, Michael Douglas, Rupert Murdoch, Gwyneth Paltrow, Elton John and Luciano Pavarotti - who acknowledged his proportions by booking two seats. Or maybe Barbra Streisand, who once memorably claimed it was the shape of her splendid nose that inspired Concorde's designers. "They should have called the plane the Streisand," she said. Or perhaps your seat was previously occupied by Sting (Mr Gordon Sumner as he usually appeared on the passenger list), who said of his favourite aircraft: "I feel

Prime Minister Margaret Thatcher visits the flight deck during a flight.
[© Adrian Meredith]

Prince Charles and Princess Diana arrive on Concorde at Heathrow Airport for the opening of Terminal 4, 1986.
[© Adrian Meredith]

James Callaghan

Valéry Giscard d'Estaing

Pope John Paul II

Jacques Chirac

Edward Heath

Georges Pompidou

Harold Wilson

François Mitterrand

safer on Concorde than I do on the M3. It's a huge gas-guzzling machine and yet it's beautiful. I love that paradox."

But it was still Sir David Frost who could claim to be the best-known regular user - although the most-travelled Concorde passenger was, in fact, the British oil tycoon Fred Finn who clocked 718 flights. Pascal Le Borgne, a French businessman, logged more than 400 trips to become Air France's most frequent Concorde flyer.

It was generally agreed that the front of the aircraft was the best place to be: on the New York run, for example, regulars vied for window seat 1D. Sir Da-vid, however, in a smooth act of reverse snobbism, favoured row 23. There, with a bit of luck, he would find fewer passengers, and thus more space for him to enjoy a supersonic snooze. Concorde was always popular among world leaders and politicians. The heads of France and Britain flew her many times. French presidents Georges Pompidou, Valéry Giscard d'Estaing, and François Mitterrand regularly used Concorde as their flagship aircraft on official state visits. James Callaghan became the first British premier to go superson-ic when he went to meet President Jimmy Carter in Washington to negotiate

Margaret Thatcher

Henry A. Kissinger

Tony Blair

Princess Margaret

Prince Charles

Prince Andrew

Sir David Frost

Dame Elizabeth Taylor

landings rights for Concorde in the United States. It was enthusiastically used by subsequent prime ministers, including Margaret Thatcher, John Major and Tony Blair (who once privately chartered Concorde to take him to Washington for discussions with President George W. Bush). The Queen used Concorde for her trip to Barbados on her Silver Jubilee in 1977 and subsequent flights including a state visit to the United States in 1991. Pope John Paul II flew to Africa on an Air France Concorde in May 1989.

French film star Catherine Deneuve was a frequent Concorde flyer for many years.
[© Moviestore Collect. Ltd / Alamy Stock Photo]

Special and Bizarre Moments

Besides conveying the world's leaders on serious matters of state, this wonderful aircraft had its more bizarre moments. A high society hostess, desperate to get a box of her favourite Mayfair chocolates to her party in New York in time, paid £2,500 for a seat for the sweets. On one early flight, when the Mach meter on the bulkhead stopped working, a worried aristocratic passenger - the late Margaret, Duchess of Argyll - started bashing it with her handbag.

Concorde enjoyed her moments in sporting history, too. Graham 'Suggs' McPherson, the lead singer of pop group Madness, claimed a record for the world's longest putt when he hit a golf ball down Concorde's aisle and which travelled five miles in twelve seconds. The golfer Sam Torrance who always tried to book seat 1A - the Queen's and Princess Diana's favourite - felt such a romantic attachment to Concorde that during lunch on one trip he proposed to Suzanne, his wife-to-be. He certainly was not the only one who had this idea. Many flight attendants remember that over the years, once the display in the cabin had reached

Mach 2, many men proposed to their sweethearts and celebrated their future marriage with a glass of champagne served by a smiling flight attendant.

Although he was not a great fan of flying, the late Beatle George Harrison loved Concorde and once gave an impromptu concert for passengers in the Concorde lounge at JFK Airport in New York with a medley of old Beatles hits. Sir Paul McCartney liked to take his favourite small guitar as hand luggage and was known - when given enough encouragement by other passengers - to start strumming some of his favourite songs in mid-air at supersonic speed. He said that one of his most enjoyable experiences on Concorde was with his then-wife Heather - who had never flown supersonically before - on her first flight when they began going out together.

Although the world's movers and shakers all have a souvenir of their times on Concorde tucked away somewhere in a drawer – one of those delightful photograph frames, or Smythson memo pads – there is no doubt that every one of them misses the beautiful machine.

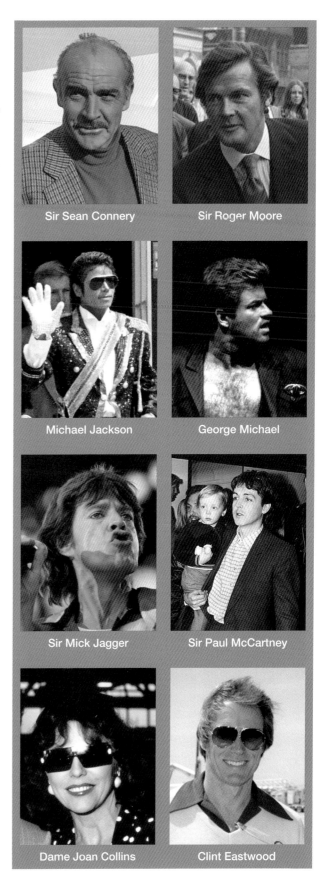

Sir Sean Connery

Sir Roger Moore

Michael Jackson

George Michael

Sir Mick Jagger

Sir Paul McCartney

Dame Joan Collins

Clint Eastwood

MEMORABLE MOMENTS AND ANECDOTES

"The only thing that tells you that you're moving is that occasionally when you're flying over the subsonic aircraft you can see all these Boeing 747s 20,000 feet below you, almost appearing to be going backwards."

– John Hutchinson, former BA Concorde captain

[© John Hutchinson]

"My most memorable experience was to be on the crew of a royal flight when HM The Queen paid a state visit to the United States of America in May 1991. I was very honoured and privileged to be one of the captains involved in that. With the American TV networks covering every step of this royal trip, it was phenomenal advertising for the 'U.K. Limited'. HRH Prince Philip joined us on the flight deck as we flew back to London."

"I had one exciting incident which was an engine surge at Mach 2 while flying from Washington to London. It felt like being in a crash. An engine surge is a disruption of the air flow to the engine resulting in a loss of thrust. There can be various causes for this. Concorde was designed to take it – she was a very strongly built aircraft. I carried out the first action of the engine surge drill by closing all four throttles which stopped all the banging and shaking, thus enabling the aircraft to return to a smooth flight. However, when doing this at Mach 2, the deceleration is quite dramatic: the cabin crew and trolleys come and join you on the flight deck, to give you a helping hand! After going through the drill

HM Queen Elizabeth II and Prince Philip disembark Concorde at Bergstrom AFB, Texas, on their state visit to the USA in 1991.
[© SRA Jerry Wilson / US Dept. of Defense]

with my flight engineer, we decided to carefully open up the throttles again and everything was fine, thus enabling us to resume Mach 2 and continue our flight to London. After landing in Heathrow, I went to the front door to say goodbye to everybody. And this was a sight I will never forget: our passengers had drunk the aircraft completely dry and I tell you, Concorde carried a lot of alcohol and they had drunk it all – the gin, the Scotch, the vodka, the champagne, the red wine, the white wine, the cognac, and anything else they could get their hands on. The passengers disembarked Concorde in a state of alcohol-fuelled euphoria, thanking me very much for a wonderful flight."

"I once flew a lady from Newcastle who was a hundred years old and who had never flown before. She had decided to fly at least once before she died and if there was any one aircraft to do it on, it had to be Concorde. We did an 'around the bay flight' which meant that we took off at Heathrow, passed the coastline near Land's End in western England, climbed to 60,000 feet, flew supersonically over the sea, and landed at Heathrow again. The poor, dear lady had to be helped off the aircraft at the end of the flight because she had so much champagne that she could not walk steadily."

–John Hutchinson, former BA Concorde captain

```
QU JFKKOBA
.NYCXGXA 171650
POS
FI BAW9002
DT NYC JW C 171645 04
-  TO THE PRESIDENT OF US AS WE FLY SOUTH I WOULD LIKE EXPRESS
HEARTLFELT THANKS ON BEHALF OF PRINCE PHILLIP AND MYSELF FOR A
WONDERFUL VISIT TO WASHINGTON.  WE SHALL NEVER FORGET THE
FRIENDLINESS WITH WHICH YOU AND MRS BUSH LOOKED AFTER US
NOR THE WARMTH OF OUR WELCOME THROUGHOUT OUR STAY.

     WE LOOK FORWARD KEENLY TO SEEING YOU AGAIN IN LONDON IN JULY

     ELIZABETH R
**NOTE RLA TO JFK AND LHR OPS**


     MAY171649 AIW 525
     @NNNN
```

Radio message from HM Queen Elizabeth II to President George H. W. Bush.
[© John Hutchinson]

"I am a pilot and therefore my best memory is a flying memory. We returned from Cayenne with an almost empty Concorde. I was in charge of the take-off from Dakar to Paris. The aircraft was light and I kept the reheats on all the way from take-off to Mach 1.7, the beginning of the supersonic cruise. Under these conditions the climbing angle was close to 20° and it was very impressive. We reached Mach 1.7 and a height of 43,000 feet about twelve minutes after take-off."

[© Pierre Grange]

– Pierre Grange, former AF Concorde pilot

"One of the flights that particularly left an impression on me was a flight departure with Michael Jackson. Concorde had to make an emergency stop during take-off, and this abandoned departure finally prompted our star to choose a subsonic flight. I recall another memorable moment with an elderly lady who went on a supersonic flight with Concorde as a gift from her family. This was a flight that took off from Paris, flew over the Atlantic to reach Mach 2 and returned to Paris. After the flight, I was present when her family asked: 'So Granny, how was it?' The lady responded: 'It was great; there are buses going back and forth, so you can get on the aircraft!'"

[© Frank Debouck]

– Frank Debouck, former AF Concorde manager

Suzanne O'Donoghue's mother enjoying her supersonic flight on Concorde.
[© Suzanne O'Donoghue]

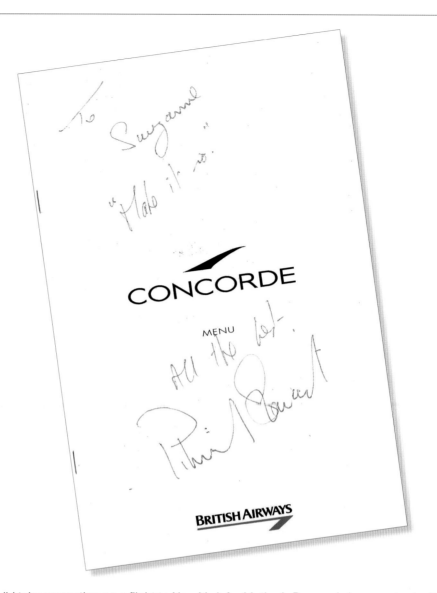

"I did take my mother on a flight to New York for Mother's Day, and she was also invited onto the flight deck for landing. She flew back on a Boeing 747, so it was expected that I would be back at London Heathrow long before her. When we took off on Concorde we had an engine problem so we had to dump all our fuel and go back to JFK Airport, New York and wait for it to be fixed. By the time we eventually arrived at Heathrow my mother was waiting for me.

"Meeting my hero Sir Patrick Stewart would be my most memorable experience. I was busy seating passengers on a flight going to New York, I turned around and there he was standing in front of me! I put my hands to my face and said, "Oh Patrick." He very quickly did exactly the same and said, "Oh Suzanne." He was an absolute delight to fly with. My fellow crew members knew how much I liked him and played a joke on me in the front galley. I even believe I said that I loved him so much that I would drink his bath water, just as he opened the toilet door that I was standing next to – he had heard every word! As crew we were not supposed to ask for autographs but my in-charge crew member who had set me up, did ask and I am happy to report that I am now the proud owner of a signed Concorde menu; I even got a kiss. That definitely is a personal memory."

– Suzanne O'Donoghue,
    former BA Concorde flight attendant

"One day I was on the late shift from 14:30 to 22:50. I was asked to meet a Concorde coming back from New York empty. She taxied on to the stand and we put on ground power and a set of steps at the front passenger door for the crew to disembark. I went up to the front door to debrief the flight engineer on the aircraft's technical state. He then told me not to go up to the flight deck as there was a special guest there, who wanted to spend a few moments on his own. Fifteen minutes later, this special guest emerged from the flight deck and to my amazement I found myself shaking hands with Brian Trubshaw, Concorde's British test pilot. We knew each other well from our days at the Fairford Flight Test Centre. Brian told me that this had been his last flight as a pilot on Concorde. He was delighted that I had met the aircraft and also that I was still working on this special fleet – it was a most memorable moment."

– Philip Cairns, former BA Concorde ground engineer

Ground engineer Philip Cairns (right) with Brian Trubshaw.
[© Philip Cairns]

"Having the opportunity to fly Concorde was not only a dream come true, it was the experience of a lifetime. I didn't fly on her for business or for leisure – I flew on her purely to experience a living, breathing machine that was capable of rocketing you to enormous speed while gracefully cutting through the stratosphere. For me it wasn't a choice – there was something primal within me that forced me to book a $7,000 roundtrip ticket on the day her retirement was announced in 2003. I simply had to fly on her.

– Johnathan Safford, American Concorde passenger

[© Johnathan Safford]

"One day, for a flight from Washington to Mexico, an elegant couple came aboard Concorde. She was wearing an evening dress and he was in a dinner jacket. We served a light dinner and I was busy serving the row in front of the couple when I saw him holding an opened bottle of red Bordeaux, and before I could help him put it back on the trolley, he dropped it. We asked him to follow us to the rear galley and told him that the best thing to do was to wash his shirt. So we did. In the meantime we handed him a blanket; he asked for a knife, made a big hole in the middle and put it on like a Peruvian poncho. He went back to his seat with applause from the rear cabin … and to his wife's displeasure. Washing the shirt was easy but drying it was quite a problem. We decided to open the oven – the galley was so warm that we almost suffocated – but the shirt came out white and neat. He thanked us and before landing he handed us a note with the words: 'I knew Air France had a very good service … but I did not know they had an excellent laundry!'"

– Annick Moyal, former AF Concorde flight attendant

"The annual C of A test flights were always memorable, during which the aircraft would do a 'flat' acceleration from Mach 2 to Mach 2.1 at around 55,000 feet – the overspeed warning systems were deliberately disabled for these occasions – and the aircraft would then proceed to do a steep zoom climb all the way up to 63,000 feet, at which point the throttles were reduced to idle and the aircraft to do a gentle 'bunt' manoeuvre, where a parabolic arc was flown, giving the illusion of being weightless for several seconds. I used to throw my pen into the air and watch it float in mid-air.

"On another test flight, we were over the Bay of Biscay, watching two French Air Force Mirages 20,000 feet below us attempting a practice intercept on us. I watched the contrails as the aircraft seemed to close on us, but the Mirages soon gave up: they just didn't have the ability to get close enough for an intercept before running out of fuel. On so many of these occasions I would sit in absolute wonder, thinking 'Is this an airliner?'

"I remember on one occasion we had a delayed departure due to a technical defect. Two young boys were running up and down the cabin, and were in the way of my team that were sorting out the problem and so I sought out their father and asked him the 'calm the kids down a bit', that father being Mick Jagger who apologized to me profusely and in no uncertain terms told the boys to sit down. Concorde defined my career in aviation, and even brought my lovely wife Liz and I together. She still is the gift that keeps on giving for us."

– Ricky Bastin, former BA Concorde ground engineer

"My most telling encounter was with Sir Harold Macmillan who was flying out to Singapore en route I believe to China. After landing at Bahrain he was allowed to stay on board with his valet. I realized that this would be the only chance I would ever have of meeting him. So without telling anybody who might have said 'no', I went back to introduce myself. I said clearly that I was the First Officer Christopher Orlebar; he replied with equal clarity, as if I did not know, that he was Harold Macmillan. Since he had been the British Prime Minister in 1962 when the treaty was signed with France to build a supersonic airliner, I thought it fair to ask why there had not been a production line for Concorde 'as long as your arm'. He immediately replied, 'American jealousy, my dear boy, American jealousy.'" (*Mach 2* magazine, issue April 2017)

– Christopher Orlebar, former BA Concorde pilot

Captain Derek Woodley recalls an anecdote about the 1996 air show in Jakarta, Indonesia: "Concorde Alpha Delta remained in the static display for the duration of the show. Visits on board were restricted for security reasons. Pilots of many nationalities were very keen to have a look at our flight deck, especially some Russian MiG-29 and Sukhoi 30 pilots, who asked some very searching questions. Hmmm!" (*Mach 2* magazine, issue April 2017)

– Derek Woodley, former BA Concorde captain

"Having made my flight on the occasion of a 'supersonic loop' from Roissy (Paris), without luggage and with a lower fuel quantity than a transatlantic flight, the takeoff was really a powerful moment with an impressive acceleration. Something had slipped out of the pocket in front of my seat; I tried to get up and pick it up ... it was impossible with the force of this acceleration that 'stuck' me to the seat. Another striking memory is the colour of the sky – a very deep blue, almost as if we were on the edge of space. We wore tuxedos, with glasses of champagne in hands and our thoughts turned to Chuck Yeager in his flight suit with helmet and mask, shaken like a leaf aboard his experimental aircraft Bell X-1 'Glamorous Glennis'."

– Philippe Gebarowski, French Concorde passenger
  and Le Bourget aviation museum volunteer

"In the summer of 1985 The Queen Mother celebrated her eighty-fifth birthday at St Paul's Walden, the home of her family line, the Bowes-Lyon family. Among the 400 people attending the event were John Hutchinson and his wife Sue. The Queen Mother who just had flown with Concorde a few days earlier, as this had been a birthday present to her from British Airways, praised the flight as a fantastic experience. John Hutchinson was introduced to her during the event. He recalls an interesting anecdote: "After asking me if I had been one of the pilots on her birthday flight (which I had not) she remarked, 'You do know that when you are landing at Heathrow on a particular runway you are flying right in front of my London home, Clarence House?' I replied, 'Yes, ma'am, I am aware of that.' She then said, 'One of your flights comes in about the time for my first gin and tonic of the evening. Well, whenever you are using that particular runway and if I am at Clarence House, I always come to the window with my gin and tonic and wave to you.' And I looked at her and said, 'You don't really, do you?' She said, 'Yes, I do because I love that aircraft so much.' I replied, 'I'll tell you what I will do from now on: if I am ever coming in to land on that runway and if the weather is good, I will flash my landings lights at you as I fly past and waggle my wings.' My great sadness is that I never sent a message to Clarence House to ask if she had seen me doing this."

– John Hutchinson, former BA Concorde captain

"I was the captain of an Air France B-747 on a flight eastbound to Paris de Gaulle Airport in October 2002. The air traffic controller simply gave us a 'traffic information' – a British Airways Concorde flight was close to us, passing us on our right side. Within seconds, we could see this magnificent aircraft flying a few hundred meters above us. It was the first time I saw a Concorde in flight at cruising altitude. What a wonderful sight! The curves of the so-called 'gothic delta wing', the long and narrow fuselage, the white colour in that very specific light at high altitude, the contrails rushing behind the engines – these images will be etched in my memory forever. I was also totally surprised by the speed of this superb aircraft, so that I glanced at my instrument panel. Yes, I was flying at normal cruising speed, close to 560 mph (900 kph), not sitting in an armchair on the ground! Within a minute, she was gone, out of view, but even years later I still remember this moment. This was part of Concorde's magic."

– Alain Rolland, former Boeing 747 captain

AU REVOIR AND FAREWELL

"*Once you have tasted flight, you will forever walk the Earth with your eyes turned skyward, for there you have been, and there you will always long to return.*"

– Leonardo da Vinci

Tragedy and Comeback

Since her first commercial flights in 1976, Concorde had become a common, yet always admired sight at airports around the world. Although seen as a white elephant in the early 1970s, Concorde not only became an icon of French and British prestige, she also generated considerable revenue for both Air France and British Airways as a commercial airliner and charter aircraft, flying to more than 350 international destinations. For many Concorde lovers – professionals

The memorial at Charles de Gaulle Airport Paris honouring the 113 crash victims of flight AF 4590. A second memorial was established near the crash site at Gonesse.
[© Hubert Michaut]

and enthusiasts alike – it seemed that the dream would last forever.

On 25 July 2000, however, as Air France Concorde F-BTSC, known as Sierra Charlie (Flight AF 4590), sped down the runway at Charles De Gaulle Airport in Paris to take off for New York, one of her wheels struck a 16-inch piece of titanium alloy that had been lost by a Continental Airlines McDonnell Douglas DC-10-30 taking off a few minutes earlier, thus shredding one of Concorde's tyres. According to the official report from the French Bureau d'Enquêtes Accidents, "in all probability" the debris from this tyre blowout pounded the nearby left wing, sending reverberations through the fuel tanks powerful enough to rupture them and causing a deadly stream of ignited aviation fuel.

The subsequent fire and engine failure caused the aircraft to crash into a hotel in nearby Gonesse shortly after takeoff, killing all hundred passengers and nine crew aboard and four in the hotel. AF 4590 was a charter flight organized by the German company Peter Deilmann Cruises, and the passengers were on their way to board the cruise ship MS Deutschland at New York City for a sixteen-day cruise. This was the only fatal accident in Concorde's history. The causes and circumstances for this tragedy remain very controversial to this day

which are subject to various books, papers, investigations, and debates.

Shortly after the loss of Sierra Charlie, the remaining Concordes of both Air France and British Airways were grounded. Safety improvements were made in the wake of the crash, including Kevlar lining on the fuel tanks, specially developed burst-resistant tyres, and more secure electrical controls. In January and April 2001, two test flight campaigns were conducted by EADS at Istres in southern France in order to validate the modifications and to certify the newly developed Michelin NZG tyre. The French test-flight crew consisted of Test Pilot Pierre Grange (Concorde pilot from 1984–89) and Airbus Test Flight Engineer Didier Ronceray, with the assistance of Air France's Concorde Chief Pilot Edgard Chillaud and Flight Engineer Roger Béral.

The first airline flight with the modifications was piloted by BA Concorde Chief Pilot Mike Bannister on 17 July 2001 and was declared a success. The first flight with passengers, all of them BA employees, took place on a fateful day: 11 September 2001. With many Concorde customers having their offices in the World Trade Center, about forty of them perished that day.

Both Air France and British Airways resumed their normal commercial operations to New York on 7 No-

vember 2001 using Sierra Delta (F-BTSD) and Alpha Echo (G-BOAE). André Turcat, captain of Concorde's maiden flight in 1969, was on board Sierra Delta that day and gave a speech to his fellow passengers in which he expressed his unshakeable confidence in Concorde's design as well as his faith that mankind could overcome any technological challenge.

Alain Verschuere, who joined Air France in 1982 and became a Concorde purser ten years later, remembers: "I had the great privilege to be a crew member on the 'rebirth flight'. Our passengers included Air France's president, Jean-Cyril Spinetta, and the French transport minister. Later the American newspaper headlines read, 'SHE IS BACK', showing a photo of our Concorde! The British Concorde touched down one hour later as Air Traffic Control could not manage two Concordes landing at the same time." New York mayor, Rudy Giuliani, later came on board Alpha Echo and greeted the passengers and jokingly asked them "to spend a lot of money during the visit". In 1976, New Yorkers had tried to 'lock out' Concorde, but now she received the warmest of welcomes, as major airports were now grateful for any aircraft arriving after the 9/11 attacks that had so widely shattered the public's trust of air travel.

Sierra Charlie (F-BTSC) painted in a special livery while in use for the 1979 movie Airport '79: The Concorde. She carried Pope John Paul II to Africa in 1989 but was destroyed in a crash after take-off from Paris CDG Airport on 25 July 2000, killing 113 people. Air France Concorde purser Alain Verschure: "The 25th of July 2000 will forever be a date of mourning. The unthinkable happened: Concorde crashed with German tourists on board. I was a stand-by purser for this flight .... my lucky star protected me."
[© Airbus / Inset: © Alain Verschuere]

The End of an Era

On 10 April 2003, both Air France and British Airways announced they would retire their Concorde fleets later that year, citing low passenger numbers following the 2000 crash, the slump in air travel following 9/11, and rising maintenance costs. In the twenty-seven years since Concorde had first roared into the hearts of people around the world, the Queen of the Skies had remained the only supersonic aircraft to fly commercially. Although the number of people travelling by air had soared, it was falling ticket prices, made possible by the wide-body airliner Boeing 747 with hundreds of seats, rather than the need for speed that drove growth within the aviation market.

In order for Concorde to fly at twice the speed of sound, she had to sacrifice fuel efficiency thus making her a fast yet expensive aircraft for an airline to run. Concorde travelling over longer distances could have addressed this problem in some way, but the sonic boom meant her flight path was limited to flying over oceans and lightly populated areas. Both Air France and British Airway had to acknowledge the financial realities of trying to run a supersonic service in an unsustainable economic climate. The announcement to withdraw Concorde from service brought a rush of bookings as many Concorde lovers wanted to get a last or once-in-a-lifetime opportunity to fly on the icon.

"Concorde, you are the magic aircraft that had us dreaming for twenty-seven years ... You've been nailed to the ground, but you will fly eternally in our hearts ..."

– Extract from the Air France guestbook

The French Au Revoir

Captain Jean-François Michel, head of Air France's Concorde division, commanded the last Air France flight from New York to Paris.
[© Jean-Philippe Lemaire]

Air France decided to end its Concorde services on 31 May 2003, with two flights on that memorable day – the last-ever flight from New York JFK back to Paris CDG and a charter flight from CDG around the Bay of Biscay.

As Sierra Delta (F-BTSD) got ready to take off from New York for the last time, airport fire trucks sprayed red, white and blue water in an arch to salute the aircraft. The flight crew consisted of Captain Jean-François Michel, head of Air France's Concorde division, First Officer Patrick Delangle, and Flight Engineer Bernard Collette. Sierra Delta took off at 08:15 local time. During the flight, Caroline Cadier, a Concorde flight attendant since 1987, had to fight back the tears when she made an announcement to the sixty-eight passengers on board: "It's now 29 years that Concorde has flown faster than the sun. One day, we do hope you'll be proud to say, I was on the last flight of this beautiful white bird." After a flight time of 3 hours and 45 minutes, Captain Michel touched down in Paris for the last time, at 16:30.

Frank Debouck, Air France's former Concorde manager, was on board: "I was asked by the president of the company to be a passenger on the last round trip to New York and back to Paris. The flight to New York on 30 May was a very happy one but the flight back was sad as the aircraft was going to land for the last time. The reception at Charles de Gaulle Airport was very emotional - the aircraft was greeted by firefighters under beautiful water jets and all available Air France staff applauded Concorde."

Twenty minutes before Sierra Delta's arrival, Concorde Fox Bravo (F-BVFB) took off at 16:10 for the last-ever ninety-minute charter flight around the Bay of Biscay. The flight crew, carrying a hundred Concorde lovers, consisted of Captain Jean-Louis Châtelain, First Officer Béatrice Vialle, and Flight Engineer M. Vasseur. When Fox Bravo, after her last thrilling supersonic flight, finally landed at 17.35, tricolours, 'Concorde Lovers' and 'J'aime Concorde' banners were being waved enthusiastically.

Sierra Delta (F-BTSD) takes off from New York for the last time, on 31 May 2003.
[© Art Brett]

Annick Moyal who had worked as an Air France Concorde flight attendant from 1978 to 1989 did not want to miss this event. She remembers the crowds and the cars blocking the motorway leading to the airport as everyone wanted to see the two Air France Concordes landing at the end of their last commercial flights: "With tears in my eyes and with hundreds of my colleagues, I watched Béatrice Vialle, the only female Air France Concorde pilot, landing Fox Bravo. I was waving a French flag and hundreds of people were applauding. Our friends who had died in the tragic accident in Gonesse in 2000 had all loved Concorde so much that they would have been so happy to see those two Concordes landing for the last time. It was a unique experience."

First Officer Béatrice Vialle, who later became a captain on the Boeing 747 and 777, will always cher-ish that moment on board the 'bel oiseau blanc': "After landing we taxied very slowly to share as long as possible the final moments of Concorde's exceptional career and thank all those who had contributed to her success and prestige throughout the world. The experience made a profound impression on me, something that still lives with me today."

When Sierra Delta and Fox Bravo dipped their noses in salute to the crowds during this emotional farewell, thus bringing the era of Air France Concorde services to an end, many spectators had tears in their eyes. In June 2003 four Concordes were flown to various museums (F-BTSC had been destroyed in the 2000 crash and F-BVFD broken up in 1994), while Fox Fox (F-BVFF) was mounted on stilts at Charles de Gaulle Airport, so air travellers can see her as they land and take off.

Captain Jean-Louis Châtelain and First Officer Béatrice Vialle wave to the crowds at CDG Airport Paris after Fox Bravo's last commercial flight.
[© Michel Thorigny]

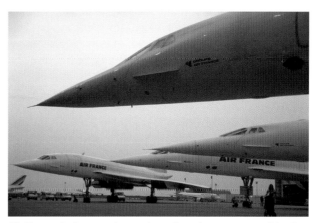

Air France's Concordes gathered on the tarmac at Charles de Gaulle Airport Paris on 31 May 2003.
[© Alexandra Jolivet]

"Concorde is an aircraft that goes faster and higher than others. I qualified on Concorde in 1999 – a dream for any young man. I never imagined making the last-ever commercial Air France Concorde flight back from New York. Many pilots put Concorde as their first choice. Concorde is an aircraft that demands to be piloted."

– Jean-François Michel, former head of Air France's Concorde division

Fox Alpha's Last Transatlantic Flight

By 1989, twenty years after Concorde's maiden flight, airline executives realized that she would not fly forever. Therefore, Air France made a promise to give one of its Concordes to the American Smithsonian Institution, home to the National Air and Space Museum. In April 2003, Air France confirmed that the Smithsonian would receive Fox Alpha (F-BVFA) in June. The museum's curator of air transportation, Dr Robert van der Linden, was available to represent the Smithsonian on Concorde's retirement flight AF 4386 on 12 June: "I was thrilled to learn that we would receive Fox Alpha, the pride of the Air France fleet."

Captain Jean-François Michel, head of Air France's Concorde division, First Officer Gérard Duval, and Flight Engineer Jean-Yves Dronne were in the cockpit. Gérard Duval who had started his aviation career as a flight engineer on various subsonic airliners, eventually became a pilot for the Boeing 727, the Airbus A310 and finally fulfilled his dream of becoming a Concorde co-pilot in 1999. He would have the honour of taking Fox Alpha to the skies for her final flight, while Captain Jean-François Michel would take her across the Atlantic and land her at Washington Dulles. Gérard remembers: "When arriving at the aircraft I noticed that the atmosphere was unusual. A small group of maintenance mechanics, who were not on duty, were watching their colleagues preparing Fox Alpha while waiting for her departure. After our flight attendants had prepared the cabin for the flight, most of them went off to attend the welcome event for the sixty passengers which included the Minister of Transport, Gilles de Robien; the President of Air France, Jean-Cyril Spinetta; CEO Pierre-Henri Gourgeon; and five former presidents of Air France. Mstislav Rostropovich, the famed Russian cellist who always flew Concorde with his cello in an adjacent seat, was to make the flight as well. Jean-François invited Minister Gilles de Robien to sit in the jump seat on the flight deck during take-off."

While Gérard Duval and his crew were preparing Fox Alpha for her final flight, scheduled to leave Paris Charles de Gaulle at noon, Robert van der Linden arrived at the Concorde lounge: "Air France had created a beautiful waiting area with all the amenities. I checked in and received my ticket, along with a luggage tag and a special commemorative package. I had walked into a party: champagne was everywhere. Several French passengers stressed to me how honoured they felt that the Smithsonian was accepting one of their Concordes. The aircraft had occupied a place in the hearts of the French people, and they felt both great pride and great sadness that the end had finally come. At 11:30 the party moved from the lounge through a check-

Fox Alpha's final flight on 12 June 2003 was also Gérard Duval's last flight with Concorde.
[© Gérard Duval]

Left: One after another, all Concordes were flown to their new homes at museums around the world.
[© Jean-Philippe Lemaire]

point and down a walkway to the waiting airliner, which was parked outside the window of the lounge for all to see and photograph one last time." After she had been pushed back from the gate, she gracefully taxied past the terminal. Gérard Duval remembers this emotional moment: "There were hundreds of people waving goodbye – or rather farewell – to Fox Alpha … knowing that she would not come back."

Robert van der Linden recalls the take-off from runway 08L: "After getting take-off clearance, Michel lit the afterburners (reheats) for thirty seconds, and Concorde responded by accelerating down the runway to 225 mph; after rolling less than 5,000 feet, we were airborne. As we climbed, she continued to accelerate, and after nineteen minutes, we reached the French coast." Fox Alpha, now clear of populated countryside, again ignited her four reheats and continued her acceleration and climb. Gérard Duval remembers a 'rendezvous' in mid-air: "During this phase we were accompanied by a Dassault Mirage 2000 fighter jet on our left, a final salute from our Armée de l'Air Française to Fox Alpha. The jet would escort us up to a speed of Mach 1.3 until it returned to its base.

During the climb, Robert van der Linden's eyes were glued to the Mach meter on the forward cabin bulkhead: "I watched as our speed increased, antic-

ipating some kind of bump that would signify we had gone supersonic. I was pleasantly disappointed. As one would expect, the cabin service was superb. Catherine Pellerin, a Concorde cabin crew instructor, was responsible for my section. I was sitting next to Pierre Giraudet, who had been the president of Air France when the Concorde entered service in 1976. He was polite but demanding of Pellerin, who responded with great attention and a caring smile for her former boss. While dinner was being prepared, Pellerin brought caviar and champagne. Monsieur Giraudet explained to me in broken English that it was just unthinkable to serve champagne with caviar. What did I know? I'm a middle-class civil servant from the suburbs. Apparently, caviar should only be accompanied by vodka. I'll remember that next time. Next came an hors d'oeuvre, a choice between medallions of rock lobster with crab sauce or foie gras with chutney and carrot jelly. I chose the lobster, which was accompanied by a white wine. I noticed that my window was quite warm, and I could feel heat radiating from the fuselage." As the flight continued peacefully, Gérard Duval handed Fox Alpha's controls over to Captain Jean-François Michel, while chatting with some of the passengers: "After finishing their meals, some passengers visited

Fox Alpha was the flagship of Air France's Concorde fleet. She was the first Concorde in service with the airline and the one with the most flight time – 17,824 hours.
[© Air France Museum]

the cockpit before our deceleration and descent."

While Robert enjoyed his dessert – seasonal fruit timbale, petits fours, and a selection of fine cheeses – Fox Alpha began her descent. Pitched high and her nose lowered for a better view, she made a straight-in approach and landed smoothly – for the last time – after just three hours and 18 minutes of which two and 57 minutes had been supersonically. Gérard Duval remembers the warm reception: "We taxied for a quarter of an hour following a planned path in front of stands full of spectators who had come to attend the final landing of the 'Bel Oiseau Blanc'."

Though Robert van der Linden was exhilarated with his supersonic experience aboard Fox Alpha, he was saddened that it would never again fly: "Concorde was clearly superior to conventional airliners – if only you could afford the ticket. And few could, which is why we're unlikely ever to see an air-

liner like Concorde again. But at least Fox Alpha will be preserved forever."

After parking the aircraft, the passengers disembarked, leaving only her cockpit crew and flight attendants aboard. When they finally left Fox Alpha after completing the last check list to join Air France officials for a photo shoot on the port wing, they had a final look at Fox Alpha proudly standing on the tarmac – despite their sadness they knew that the flagship of Air France's Concorde fleet would be in good hands.

Gérard Duval would see his aircraft once again: "In July 2005 I visited the Steven F. Udvar-Hazy Center before attending the 17th ISNA (International Symposium on Nonlinear Acoustics) at the Pennsylvania State University. I appreciate this great museum and it was nice to see Fox Alpha again, now proudly standing alongside the Boeing 707 prototype, the Lockheed SR-71, the first space shuttle, and many other significant aircraft."

Fox Bravo – Journey to a New Home

by Hermann Layher, Director of the Sinsheim and Speyer Technik Museums

"Sinsheim is the only place in the world which is home to both Concorde and the Tupolev Tu-144."

Concorde Fox Bravo (F-BVFB) and the Russian supersonic airliner, the Tupolev Tu-144, make our Technik Museum Sinsheim in Germany unique and world famous. Most notably, both aircraft are placed in take-off position on a steel frame on the roof – a feat no other museum has yet repeated. Even from a distance you can see the two white beauties, a view that might take your breath away. In 2001, we were able to buy the Tupolev Tu-144 directly from the manufacturer, Tupolev, and bring her to our museum. Two years later, when we received Concorde, a dream came true. Every day I experience a feeling of sublime happiness when admiring these two wonderful machines.

When Fox Bravo was awarded to us in 2003, a delegation from our museum visited the Air France hangar at the Paris Charles de Gaulle Airport where all the airline's Concordes were lined up. For the last flight ever of 'our' Concorde we had four seats, the rest taken up by guests of Air France. Among them was the widow of Captain Christian Marty, the pilot of the Concorde which so tragically had crashed in 2000.

After taking off from Paris on 24 June 2003, we headed for the Atlantic where Fox Bravo – for the final time – flew at Mach 2. Then she headed to Germany. The fuel for her last flight was paid for by the museum. With us was our then vice-president, Robert Gärtner, our member of the board of directors, Michael Einkörn, as well as our camera team. Thousands of spectators where gathered at the Baden-Airpark to witness the landing. We had chosen this airport because from there the continuation of Fox Bravo's transport by barge on the Rhine would not present any obstacles in the form of bridges across the river. With the help of the French technicians, we then went to work, and for the last time started Fox Bravo's engines at 6:30 to burn the remaining fuel. When the fuel eventually ran out, the engines spat out hundred-feet-long darting flames. This was an experience you would never forget. After the removal of her wings and tail fin, Fox Bravo travelled by barge and road to the Technik Museum Sinsheim. In total, about a million people witnessed her final landing and onward transportation which went on through the night and into the morning. Unforgettable was a rave par-

Fox Bravo (F-BVFB) lands for her final time at the Baden-Airpark, Germany, on 24 June 2003.
[© Kai-jens Meyer]

Fox Bravo after the removal of her wings and tail fin.
[© Technik Museum Sinsheim / TMS]

ty at the Hockenheimring with loud music and people dancing on the autobahn bridges. Of all the transportation journeys we've done over the years, this was the most amazing of all.

After her arrival, Fox Bravo was reassembled to join the Tupolev Tu-144 already on exhibit on the museum grounds. On 17 March 2004, the 'Queen of the Skies' was positioned in take-off position on a steel frame above museum hall No. 2 of the Technik Museum Sinsheim. The Air France technicians were very helpful as were their Lufthansa colleagues who were thrilled to support us again, having assisted us in reassembling our Boeing 747 a few years

before. Thanks to their cooperation, our Concorde is now able to move her droop nose up and down again – as she did when she was still operational. It is wonderful that we were able to receive this French Concorde for the symbolic price of just one euro. Our two museums (Sinsheim and Speyer) are non-profit organizations, financed exclusively through entrance fees and donations. Therefore, twenty hours of free news broadcast by various TV stations covering our Concorde's transportation helped to increase the museum's profile. To this day, Fox Bravo is the highlight of our aircraft exhibition, and she remains the most beautiful aircraft in the world.

Transport by barge on the Rhine.
[© TMS]

Fox Bravo on the German autobahn at night.
[© TMS]

Fox Bravo (left) on display with her former rival, the Tupolev Tu-144. Sinsheim is the only place where both supersonic airliners are exhibited together.
[© TMS]

The British Farewell

British Airways decided to end its Concorde service with a farewell tour around North America and the United Kingdom with October 24 being the final day of operation that was to see the last three flights coming home to London Heathrow from New York, the Bay of Biscay, and Edinburgh.

At 14:20, Alpha Echo (G-BOAE), commanded by Captain Chris Norris, took off from Edinburgh with her passengers on a last supersonic flight over the North Sea. The flight crew also consisted of Captain

Les Brodie, Senior Flight Officer Paul Griffin, and Senior Engineering Officer Trevor Norcott. Flight attendant Iona Ferguson remembers: "The service was not the same as on a regular flight as all passengers had either won tickets through the British Airways employee raffle or been chosen as a way of thanks for special service. It was emotional in a way which is hard to describe. We announced that after landing the passengers could line up to visit the cockpit." Iona had been chosen to make the announcements

and struggled to keep her voice steady once Alpha Echo touched down: "Ladies and gentlemen, we would like to welcome you to London Heathrow. It is with great sadness and with heavy hearts we thank you for choosing to fly with us on British Airways' supersonic Concorde on this historical day and we hope you loved the experience as much as we have loved looking after you. It has been our pleasure to serve on Concorde over the years, knowing what a privilege it is, and we hope you will all remember your

Mach 2 experience today with much fondness and pride. We have no doubt that you will all miss seeing Concorde's silhouette soaring over London but it is now time for us to wish you all the very best for the future – thank you, and good night." Iona looked over at her colleague who was also in tears and yet both were smiling, knowing how incredibly lucky they were to have been such a part of such a magnificent history: "We disembarked by the hangars onto red carpets and near the other two Concordes which had

British Airways cabin service director Claire Sullivan sheds a tear on her last Concorde flight.
[© British Airways]

Concorde comes home to London Heathrow on 24 October 2003.
[© Howell Green]

come in from the final New York and the 'around the bay' flights. It was hard – so hard – to leave the aircraft. It still brings me to tears thinking about that magical yet terribly sad day."

At the same time as Alpha Echo departed Edinburgh at 14:20, Captain Paul Douglas took Alpha Fox (G-BOAF) to the skies over Heathrow for a the last-ever supersonic flight around the Bay of Biscay with a hundred VIPs and British Airways staff on board. The flight crew also included Senior Flight Officer Mark Jealous and Senior Engineering Officers Peter Carrigan and Warren Hazelby.

An enthusiastic crowd welcomes Concorde at London Heathrow on 24 October 2003.
[© John Powell / johnnypowell.net]

163

An enthusiastic crowd welcomes Concorde at London Heathrow on 24 October 2003.
[© British Airways]

"In the end, Concorde is just an aluminium tube, an aircraft, a machine. An exceptional one there is no doubt, but still only a machine. What makes her so different is her people – our customers and British Airways staff. They give her a soul. What we have learned is how to offer superior service."

– Captain Mike Bannister, former BA Concorde chief pilot

On the other side of the Atlantic, in New York, Captain Mike Bannister, British Airways' Chief Concorde Pilot, Senior First Officer Jonathan Napier, and Senior Engineering Officers David Hoyle and Robert Woodcock, were getting ready to take Alpha Golf (G-BOAG) with a full complement of VIPs on board home to London. Before the departure, the airport's firemen gave Alpha Golf a water cannon tribute of red, white and blue jets of water. The flight crew showed its appreciation by waving the U.S. flag and the Union Jack.

The Air Traffic Controller who had welcomed the first Concordes to New York in 1977 was there and radioed to Concorde: "It's been wonderful working with your aircraft – good luck to all the crews, and we're going to miss you." Concorde's flight crew replied: "It's been great knowing you and we're going to miss you a lot." Watched by thousands of Concorde lovers, Alpha Golf took off from the Big Apple for the very last time, at 17:20.

As Alpha Golf entered the United Kingdom's airspace, Air Traffic Control at London Heathrow directed Alpha Echo and Alpha Fox onto their final approaches. Alpha Golf made one final loop to overfly Heathrow and London before taking up position as the third aircraft in line. The three Concordes were greeted by crowds of people gathered on the roadsides, in carparks, and on tops of buildings. The first aircraft to land was Alpha Echo at 16:00, followed by Alpha Fox three minutes later. Finally, Alpha Golf touched down at 16:05 receiving a water cannon salute surprising the flight crew

which was waving flags out of the windows. Meanwhile, her two sisters taxied around the airport one last time. The Air Traffic Controller beamed out the message: "The eagles have landed – welcome home."

That day twenty-seven years of British Airways Concorde service ended with the five active aircraft – G-BOAA and G-BOAB had been retired since 2000 – positioned for a group photo, together with the airline's Concorde staff who had worked with the aircraft.

The Last Flight – Coming Home

The 26th of November 2003 marked the day of Concorde's last-ever flight: to fly Alpha Fox (G-BOAF) from London Heathrow to Filton, the birthplace of the British Concordes, where she would find a new home at the Aerospace Bristol aviation heritage centre. The flight crew consisted of Captains Les Brodie, Paul Douglas, and Mike Bannister, and Senior Engineer Officers Warren Hazelby and Trevor Norcott. Iona Ferguson, who was a flight attendant on one of the three final commercial flights on 24 October, was on board - this time as a passenger: "It was hard to believe that I received a passenger ticket for the last Concorde, to be flown from London to Filton where she was to stay. To be back on her – in civilian clothes this time – felt both odd and wonderful. We flew over the Clifton Suspension Bridge

and I have seen some utterly incredible photographs of what it looked like from the ground. A handful of us [crew] who were on that flight stayed [on board] as long as we possibly could before being forced to leave when we saw the bus – which was taking us back up to London – leaving! The thought of Concorde being 'mothballed' and sitting on the tarmac – regardless of how well looked after she is – breaks my heart. She was built to fly and can still do so. It is like watching a rare bird caged."

For the British Airways staff working on board or travelling as winning passengers on this last-ever Concorde flight, it was an

Concorde Alpha Fox (G-BOAF) receives a water cannon salute before her last-ever flight.
[© David Apps]

emotionally charged experience. For Catherine Murray this flight to Filton was memorable for another reason: her boyfriend, IT worker Robert Pilgrim, proposed as Alpha Fox reached Mach 2 at 60,000 feet. A stunned Catherine said: "He chose the right moment."

[© Iona Ferguson]

Alpha Fox overflies Clifton Suspension Bridge, Bristol, as thousands of enthusiasts gather to pay tribute to her on her last-ever flight.
[© Adrian Meredith Collection]

The end of an era in aviation history: Alpha Fox touches down at Filton on 26 November 2003, the last-ever landing of a Concorde.
[© Adrian Meredith]

Delta Golf at the Brooklands Museum
by Allan Winn, former Brooklands CEO

"Concorde volunteers took charge of tracking down the thousands of parts needed to complete the restoration."

Since Concorde Delta Golf (G-BBDG) was allocated by British Airways to Brooklands Museum in 2003, she has not only become an important and lastingly popular exhibit but has also fostered an extraordinary community within the museum. From the very beginning a team of volunteers grew around Delta Golf. Under their leader Gordon Roxburgh this team adopted the aircraft and became the driving workforce of its restoration and interpretation. They included aerospace engineering students from the University of Surrey as well as retired and serving engineers from British Airways. Although the physical dismantling and rebuilding of the main structure of Delta Golf was handled by a professional aircraft-dismantling company, the Concorde volunteers took charge of tracking down the thousands of parts needed to complete the restoration. This was necessary as Delta Golf had been stripped of all her useful parts over a twenty-year period as a spares source to keep the rest of the BA fleet flying.

Once the aircraft's restoration – which included painting the entire aircraft and designing the internal displays – was complete, a further team of volunteer stewards was formed to operate it as a live exhibit. But the volunteer input did not end there. Having completed a restoration of Delta Golf, which many observers had deemed impossible, the team – with further help from the University of Surrey and the UK Engineering Sciences Research Council – embarked on a further 'impossible' task: the simulator's return to service on which all British Concorde crews did their training. This included converting the machine from analogue to digital operation and building a new own-design visual system for it, and then slaving it into Microsoft Flightsim to allow it to 'fly' anywhere in the world. Once this amaz-

ing feat had been completed, the team attracted a group of twelve Concorde captains, first officers and flight engineers to operate it, giving visitors the opportunity to learn how to 'fly' this amazing aircraft. The impact on the museum has been extraordinary. Even during her two-year restoration, Delta Golf attracted new museum visitors to watch progress, but once she was formally opened by HRH Prince Michael of Kent in August 2006 she drove a massive increase in numbers. In addition to generating increased admissions revenue, Concorde also created a new revenue stream, as visitors pay a premium to take a half-hour experience which includes a welcome briefing aboard an airport ramp

Delta Golf's cockpit section before her restoration.
[© Ian Haskell]

bus, a tour of the rear cabin and then a virtual flight in the front cabin, where they experience some of the glamour of sitting in the seats and taking a flight. With over 40,000 visitors taking the half-hour Con-

corde experience each year, a further 300 or so flying the simulator and hundreds more attending special Concorde events, Concorde is generating around £250,000 a year for the museum.

Delta Golf after her full restoration, open to the public.
[© Brooklands Museum Trust Ltd]

Visiting Sierra Delta in Le Bourget

by Jean-François Louis, Association des Amis du Musée de l'Air

Museum volunteer and Concorde lover Jean-François Louis.
[© Jean-François Louis]

In 2014, I became a volunteer at the Musée de l'air et de l'espace, Le Bourget, conducting guided tours of our Boeing 747 and our two Concordes. First, I could little imagine how these tours were such a dream come true for our visitors, in particular our younger guests.

The tour usually begins in the Concorde hangar, with the people often saying: "Wow, this aircraft is beautiful! What a pity that it doesn't fly anymore." We then talk about Concorde's genesis, technology, history, rivals, before boarding both Concordes (Prototype 001 and Sierra Delta).

Visitors can be divided into three groups. Firstly, the 'worshipers' own almost everything that has been written about Concorde, and had wet eyes when watching Concorde's final flights. The second group are passionate enthusiasts and aviation professionals, keen to learn more about Concorde's genesis, her history, technology, performance, rivals, and retirement; they often ask questions about the fuel transfer, the lengthening of the fuselage in flight, and the causes for Concorde's commercial failure. The third group are 'mainstream' visitors, many of them exploring Concorde 'face to face' for the first time and who always want to learn a little more of the aircraft, its technology, and the typical passenger profiles.

The most frequent remarks relate to Concorde's beauty and I often hear the term 'majestic'. After visiting both Concordes, many visitors are astounded by the cabin size. I often hear questions like: "How did you put in a bed for the French president? Why was the price of a Paris–New York ticket so high? Will there be another Concorde soon?" Most of the visitors regret Concorde's retirement and the step backwards in terms of flight duration to New York. When our visitors leave, their heads full of dreams, many regret that they never had the opportunity to fly on such a fantastic aircraft that was so far ahead of its time.

The nose of prototype 001. Note the difference to Sierra Delta's nose. *[© Ben Wang]*

Restoring and Maintaining Concorde

The restoration and preservation of the Concordes in museums around the world requires dedicated teams of engineers, technicians, and helpers. Alexandra Jolivet worked on Air France's active Concorde fleet from late 2000 until their retirement in 2003. As a volunteer at the Le Bourget museum, Alex participated in the restoration of Concordes 001 (F-WTSS) and Sierra Delta (F-BTSD): "I set up the team with a friend who works in the museum's workshop. Over time more people joined us to help preserve Con-

corde and pass on her history to the public. Other jets are for kids!"

Museum volunteer and former Concorde engineer Alexandra Jolivet.
[© Alexandra Jolivet]

After Concorde's retirement, many spare parts and various cabin items including gauges, seats and trolleys were auctioned off to raise money for a number of charities. A nosecone fetched $490,000 at an Air France SA auction in Paris.

Sierra Delta and prototype 001 capture the imagination of the museum's visitors.
[© Musée de l'Air et de l'Espace - Le Bourget / Vincent Pandellé]

RETURN TO FLIGHT?

"The thought of her being mothballed and sitting on the tarmac – regardless of how well looked after she is – breaks my heart. Concorde was built to fly and she can still do so. It is like watching a rare bird caged."

– Iona Ferguson, former BA Concorde flight attendant

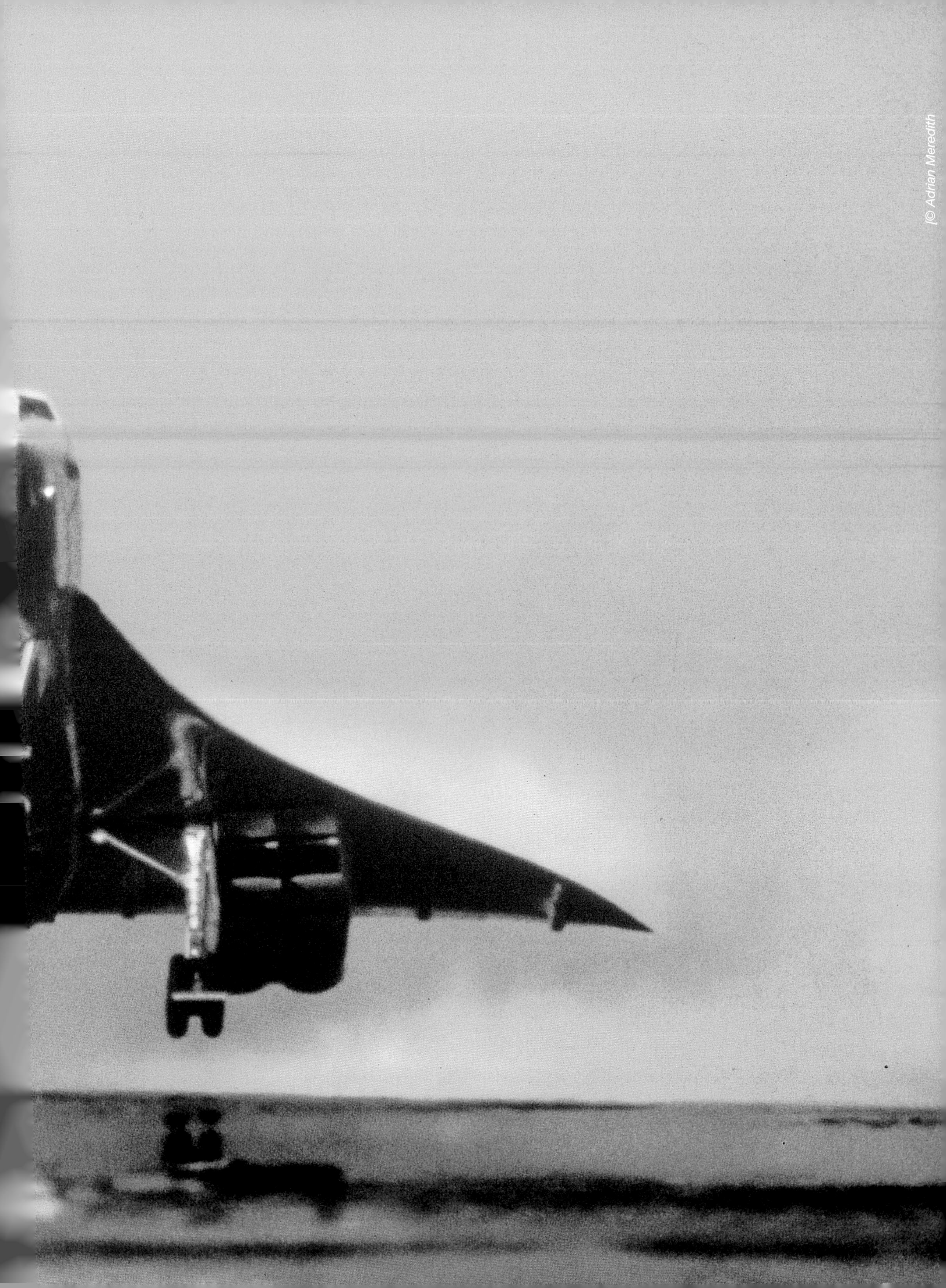
© Adrian Meredith

The history of aviation has seen many icons taking to the skies. Concorde was one of the most famous and most-loved of them all. When André Turcat and Brian Trubshaw made their successful maiden flights in 1969, they ignited a love affair that caused Concorde to capture the world's imagination. Although her flying days have come to an end, the love affair has not. Today she enjoys her status as a prestigious exhibition piece in some of the world's finest aviation museums, serving as a magnet for visitors. Standing in front of Concorde and admiring her sheer beauty and unmatched engineering, many among us – aviation professionals and enthusiasts alike – might well wonder if this marvel could ever return to the skies. Over the last few decades, numerous retired aircraft have been reactivated after painstaking restoration and testing. Among these are the famous Supermarine Spitfire, the Messerschmitt Bf 109, the North American P-51 Mustang, the Boeing B-29 Superfortress, and the Avro Vulcan. The latter was a jet-powered, tailless, delta-wing, high-altitude strategic bomber operated by the RAF from 1956 until 1984. The technologically

Vulcan XH558, the *Spirit of Great Britain*, gracefully taking off during an air show in 2008.
[© CF38]

Vulcan XH558 during a formation flight with the Red Arrows in 2015.
[© Steve Buckley, RAF/MOD]

sophisticated and complex Vulcan is part of Concorde's genealogy and her Olympus engines provided the basis for the supersonic airliner's power plant. Through a combination of public donations and lottery funding raising several million pounds, one retired Vulcan, XH558, named the *Spirit of Great Britain*, was restored to flight by the 'Vulcan To The Sky Trust' and displayed as a civilian aircraft at various air shows from 2008 until 2015, before being retired a second time for engineering reasons.

The Former Rival's Return to Flight

With regards to various historic aircraft restored to flying condition, only the Vulcan is – remotely – technically comparable to Concorde. Nevertheless, despite some similarities, Concorde's complex and unique design does place her in a league of her own. Yet, campaigners envisioning Concorde's return to the skies argue that the success of reactivating the Vulcan as a display aircraft could at least serve as an encouragement and 'template' for a potential 'Concorde cause'.

However, there is only one aircraft that comes relatively close to Concorde's design and performance: the short-lived Soviet Tupolev Tu-144, once a supersonic rival and deprecatingly dubbed by the Western press as 'Concordski'. In 1995, after an agreement was signed between IBP Aircraft, Tupolev, NASA, Rockwell, McDonnell Douglas, and Boeing, one preserved Tu-144 (S/N 77114) was extensively modified at a cost of approximately $350 million to be used as a flying testbed as part of a research programme for the second generation of supersonic air travel. Designated the Tu-144LL, with 'LL' being the abbreviation for Letayushchaya Laboratoriya – the Russian term for Flying Laboratory – the aircraft made twenty-seven successful flights during 1996 and 1997 but was retired two years later due to the lack of further funding.

With no large-scale project – sponsored by the British or French governments or any international partner – aiming to use Concorde for scientific test or research flights in sight, the enthusiasts who want to see her fly again would have to find an enormously financially potent partner or sponsor for a return-to-flight project.

Then, a well-preserved and professionally maintained Concorde adequate for restoration to flying condition with the least effort and cost, would have to be found. From the eighteen Concordes that still exist, some have been moved into hangars after their last flight and beautifully cared for, while others have spent many years outdoors, exposed to the elements and resulting in corrosive damage. The six prototypes, pre-production and production test aircraft which were retired and moved to museums during the 1970s and 1980s, do not conform to the type certificate as later defined by the fourteen production aircraft built for airline service (see more following), so they can be excluded from the list of potential candidates for a second lease of life. This limits the number to the twelve surviving aircraft used for airline service.

Roll-out of the restored Tupolev Tu-144LL in 1996. She was part of a research programme for the second generation of supersonic air travel.
[© NASA]

The Tu-144LL ready for take-off. International cooperation and funding made her restoration possible.
[© NASA]

The Tu-144LL in flight. Her role in the supersonic research programme gave her a (short-lived) second lease on life.
[© NASA]

Air France Concordes

Foxtrot Alpha (F-BVFA), the flagship of the Air France Concorde fleet, was flown to the United States in 2003 and is now on display at the Smithsonian National Air and Space Museum.
[© Gérard Duval]

With Concorde Sierra Charlie (F-BTSC) lost in the tragic crash of 2000 and Foxtrot Delta (F-BVFD) dismantled six years earlier due to corrosion, there are still five Air France aircraft in existence today. Two of them can probably be ruled out as they have been stored outside since 2003, and therefore exposed to rain and snow. One is Foxtrot Bravo (F-BVFB) at Sinsheim, Germany, the other is Foxtrot Foxtrot (F-BVFF) at Charles de Gaulle Airport, Paris. The remaining three have been stored inside. Foxtrot Alpha (F-BVFA) was flown to the American Smithsonian National Air and Space Museum in 2003 and immediately stored inside the museum without any alterations afterwards. Sierra Delta (F-BTSD) has been beautifully cared for inside the Musée de l'air et de l'espace (Air and Space Museum) at Le Bourget near Paris, since 2003. Foxtrot Charlie (F-BVFC) is stored outside at the Aeroscopia Museum at the Airbus factory in Toulouse, but is well maintained and sealed from the elements.

British Airways Concordes

All seven British Airways Concordes have survived to this day. With Alpha Bravo (G-BOAB) still in storage parked outside at Heathrow Airport, London, and stripped of much of her interior, she barely qualifies as a candidate for reactivation. The remaining six were given to various museums. Two of them are stored outdoors in the United States: Alpha Golf (G-BOAG) at the Museum of Flight, Seattle, and Alpha Delta (G-BOAD) at the Intrepid Sea, Air and Space Museum, New York. Alpha Foxtrot (G-BOAF), the last Concorde ever completed, was stored outside at Aerospace Bristol, Filton, before being moved into a hangar especially built for her in 2017. With these three aircraft exposed to the elements for years, they probably have to be ruled out as well. Alpha Alpha (B-BOAA), which was transported to the Museum of Flight, Edinburgh, Scotland, in 2004, had her wings removed in order to fit into the museum. Although later reattached, it would be very laborious and expensive to restore their structural integrity as is the case with the French Foxtrot Bravo which had to be dismantled for her transport to Sinsheim. This leaves two British Concordes which have been stored inside and wonderfully looked after: one is Alpha Echo (G-BOAE) on display at Grantley Adams International Airport in Barbados, the other Alpha Charlie (B-BOAC) at the Manchester Airport Viewing Park.

Alpha Charlie (B-BOAC), the flagship of the British Airways Concorde fleet, is now on display at the Manchester Airport Viewing Park.
[© British Airways]

Sierra Delta (F-BTSD) is a potential contender for reactivation as she has been beautifully cared for inside the Musée de l'air et de l'espace at Le Bourget. Prototype 001 is visible in the background.
[© Musée de l'Air et de l'Espace - Le Bourget / Xavier Derégel]

Contenders for Reactivation

All in all, among the eighteen surviving airframes, two from Air France (Sierra Delta in Le Bourget and Foxtrot Charlie in Toulouse) and two from British Airways (Alpha Charlie in Manchester and Alpha Echo in Barbados) are – theoretically and potentially – in a good enough physical condition to be considered for a restoration project aimed at returning one of them to flying. With regard to logistics and transportation distances for spare parts and technical personnel, Alpha Echo in Barbados would certainly require more organizational effort and therefore incur more costs than the aircraft stored in the United States or Europe. Besides determining which would be the most suited for reactivation, there are numerous monumental obstacles preventing this dream from becoming a reality which the general Concorde enthusiast might not be aware of. Returning an iconic World War II aircraft or even the more complex Avro Vulcan to the skies is one thing – Concorde quite another. Therefore, various factors would have to be examined.

Nevertheless, when the Concorde fleets were retired, none of the aircraft was properly 'mothballed' ('cocooned') with regards to potential future reactivation as is done with both retired civil and military aircraft which are stored in hangars or preservation-friendly environments such as the Mojave Desert. Therefore, a professionally 'mothballed' and properly sealed aircraft is always in a better condition than an aircraft put on display, despite how well maintained it might be.

Alpha Echo (G-BOAE) is now on display at Grantley Adams International Airport in Barbados.
[© Bob Ware]

Potential Use

With Concorde's rich history as an iconic display aircraft for air shows, royal flypasts and formation flights with the Patrouille de France or the Red Arrows, she certainly would receive an enormous amount of attention if ever used again for heritage flights. In order to operate on a viable commercial or semi-commercial basis needed to cover her massive flying and maintenance costs, Concorde would have to do what she had done so successfully in the past: flying as an exclusive charter aircraft taking fare-paying passengers to various places or offering short supersonic flights, that would make Concorde herself the destination. With only one Concorde potentially active, she would certainly enjoy tremendous international demand and could be operated by a dedicated non-profit group overseeing the process of her restoration and return to the skies.

Spare Parts and Certification

With Concorde made up of hundreds of thousands of parts, each and every part would require certification by the French and British civil aviation authorities in order to receive a certificate of airworthiness, let alone the aircraft as a whole. After her retirement, numerous spare parts – ranging from simple valves to complex machinery – were either sold, auctioned off (some of them for charitable causes) or scrapped, while others were donated to various museums and put into storage. With the operational history of many of these surviving parts unclear, they would have to be re-certified by the approved manufacturer, such as Airbus or Rolls-Royce, who originally made them. Many of the manufacturers who specialized in Concorde parts either no longer exist or have moved on to more modern technologies. Therefore, after all these years, most of the test equipment necessary to certify the required spares no longer exists and would have to be rebuilt. One example is the large number of hydraulic seals in the tanks that would all have to be replaced.

Moreover, the spare parts that are no longer available would either have to be remanufactured from scratch at significant cost or cannibalized from other Concordes on display. There are various ways of re-certifying Concorde: one being as a subsonic aircraft without passengers – the least complex – but would mean that her flights could not generate any income. The second option would be as a cargo aircraft with a small number of passengers, and the third would be her 'comeback' as a supersonic aircraft with full passenger capacity, certainly the most challenging and therefore the most expensive, yet most attractive, variant.

Support Services

In comparison to subsonic airliners Concorde was a very maintenance-intensive aircraft and therefore expensive to operate. She required, and would still require, certified fuel, hydraulic oil, fuel, fluids, ground power units, as well as support from manufacturers such as Rolls-Royce to run her powerful but complex engines.

Qualified Engineers and Technicians

Former Concorde engineers and technicians whose skills and experience are essential for the complex task of restoration would have to regain their licences to work on the aircraft as these have long since expired.

[© Adrian Meredith]

Qualified Flight Crew and Type Holder Certificate

With Concorde officially retired for good in 2003, her pilots and flight engineers have not renewed their flight certifications, these requiring regular checks and testing. Moreover, there are no official training facilities, including certified flight simulators, as they were deactivated when Concorde went out of service. However, one flight simulator has been reactivated at Brooklands Museum as a visitor attraction. The French are working to bring their simulator back to life in Toulouse, so there will eventually be two active simulators. However, both systems were removed from their hydraulic jacks, so they will never again fully operate as they did while Concorde was in service. With Airbus being the successor of BAC and Aérospatiale as the type certificate holder for Concorde, the civil aviation authorities would require Airbus to also hold the type certificate for a reactivated Concorde. With regard to Concorde's unique and still cutting-edge design, it is unlikely that Airbus would agree to a transfer of the type certificate to another aircraft manufacturer or aviation company.

Costs

Facing the enormously complex task of restoring Concorde, meeting all certification requirements and keeping her flying for several years would require a grand budget capable of covering numerous unforeseeable expenses. The costs are an unknown figure. While the reactivation of the Vulcan required several millions pounds, the Tupolev Tu-144's extensive modification and test flight operations swallowed a staggering $350 million, a sum very unlikely to be invested into a single aircraft without any scientific or military purpose in mind.

Addressing some of the key technical aspects in the restoration process of Concorde by concentrating on present-day operational requirements, Ricky Bastin, a former British Airways Concorde ground engineer, says:

"Firstly, a full structural survey would be required on the relevant airframe(s), to ensure that structural deterioration does not rule out the venture. Then, a full survey of the electrical installation would be necessary, and once electrical and then hydraulic power are established, the integrity of the various hydraulic seals will have to be established, and, where necessary, seals replaced. It is highly likely that museum aircraft would need to be cannibalized for certain spares. An engine restorative process would have to be agreed with Rolls-Royce, whose support in any venture is absolutely vital, and low to zero hours engines would possibly need to be sourced. If it is desired to use the aircraft on a semi-commercial basis, e.g. charters, then recent legislation requires that several systems would require a radical upgrade – however, fortunately there are 'off the shelf' solutions available. As an example, the INS [inertial navigation system] was seen as becoming unfit for purpose as long ago as 1999, as well as the ADS-B [automatic dependent surveillance–broadcast] and EGPWS [enhanced ground proximity warning system] systems now being mandatory for commercial aircraft. These two systems require at least a dual GPS system to be installed for them to operate:

an ADS-B is a surveillance technology in which an aircraft determines its position via satellite-based navigation and periodically broadcasts it, thus enabling it to be tracked. An EGPWS alerts pilots if their aircraft is in immediate danger of flying into the ground or an obstacle. To implement the required changes a

For reactivation Concorde would have to go through a 'D (Major) Check' which involves the careful disassembling of her major parts, extensive tests with them, as well as a structural inspection of the airframe.
[© Adrian Meredith]

great deal of weight saving can actually be achieved, equating to a lower fuel burn. The proposal is to replace two air data computers, three INS units and their equipment, as well as some other devices. These would all be replaced with a single Honeywell ADIRU [air data and inertial reference unit], together with a single SARU [standby attitude reference unit], both supplying airspeed, angle of attack and altitude as well as position and attitude information. A simple FMS [flight management system] for lateral navigation only [LNAV] would be required, the simplest solution being similar to the ARINC 629 card system used on the Boeing 777. The FMS is a fundamental component of a modern airliner's avionics that automates a wide variety of in-flight tasks, thus reducing the workload on the flight crew. The card system would also house the necessary analogue/digital and digital/analogue converters that would enable the new systems to interface with the aircraft. A major issue however becomes one of display, the simplest and cheapest long-term option being to remove most of the pilot's flight instruments, as well as the primary and secondary engine instrument panels and replace them with a total of four flat panel LCD displays – this sort of retrofit is common in North America for older-design aircraft. A full component overhaul

regime would need to be established, particularly for the 'classic' Concorde components, which would of course be costly."

Since Concorde's retirement in 2003, various organizations, most notably the 'Save Concorde Group' and 'Club Concorde', a business venture supported by former Concorde pilots, have been making efforts to make the reactivation of at least one Concorde possible. The 'Save Concorde Group', supported by members from the aviation world as well as politicians, celebrities, and the general public, even submitted a petition to the British government and Airbus UK, signed by 30,000 people, asking for their support to return Concorde to the skies. Despite widespread hope, the petition has not been favourably received.

To this day, British Airways still owns the Concordes built in Britain, thus the aircraft on public display have been loaned to the museums. Air France donated four of their remaining Concordes to museums where they are on display, the exception being Foxtrot Foxtrot (F-BVFF) which was placed on display at Paris Charles de Gaulle. Therefore, an agreement with British Airways or one of these museums would have to be reached to either buy a Concorde or obtain permission to restore and operate one and then return it to the museum after its final retirement.

Reactivating Concorde would probably require the replacement of the electrical installation as well as the integration of modern avionic systems.
[© BAE Systems]

Nevertheless, it is highly speculative that the owners would agree to give away their Concordes to such an ambitious, yet probably incalculable undertaking, as nothing similar has ever been undertaken without the leadership and funding of a player such as NASA, Boeing, Airbus or a national government.

Moreover, the Concordes donated to museums, such as Foxtrot Alpha (F-BVFA) at the Smithsonian and Sierra Delta (F-BTSD) at Le Bourget, are considered not only technological marvels or masterpieces of art but also historic artefacts that should be preserved in the layout they were originally built. Therefore, any alteration or modernization of the avionics in order to meet present-day operational requirements would compromise their historical integrity.

With the years passing and most of the 'fathers'

of Concorde who designed and built her deceased, the technical knowledge required to rebuild, maintain and fly Concorde might be gone in the not-too-distant future as engineers, technicians and pilots start fading away. Therefore, the theoretical chance of restoring her to flying condition and taking her to the skies again, seems to be slowly and irreversibly passing, if not already.

With subsonic airliners being the standard aircraft for intercontinental air travel today and for the foreseeable future, the supersonic Concorde, now gracefully enduring her fate as a prestigious museum artefact, might sadly look up to the skies as a domain she once so supremely ruled. Like all icons, Concorde's place in the popular imagination may well prove to be her enduring legacy.

Alpha Echo (G-BOAE) in her prime. It is very
unlikely that Concorde will return to the skies.
[© Art Brett]

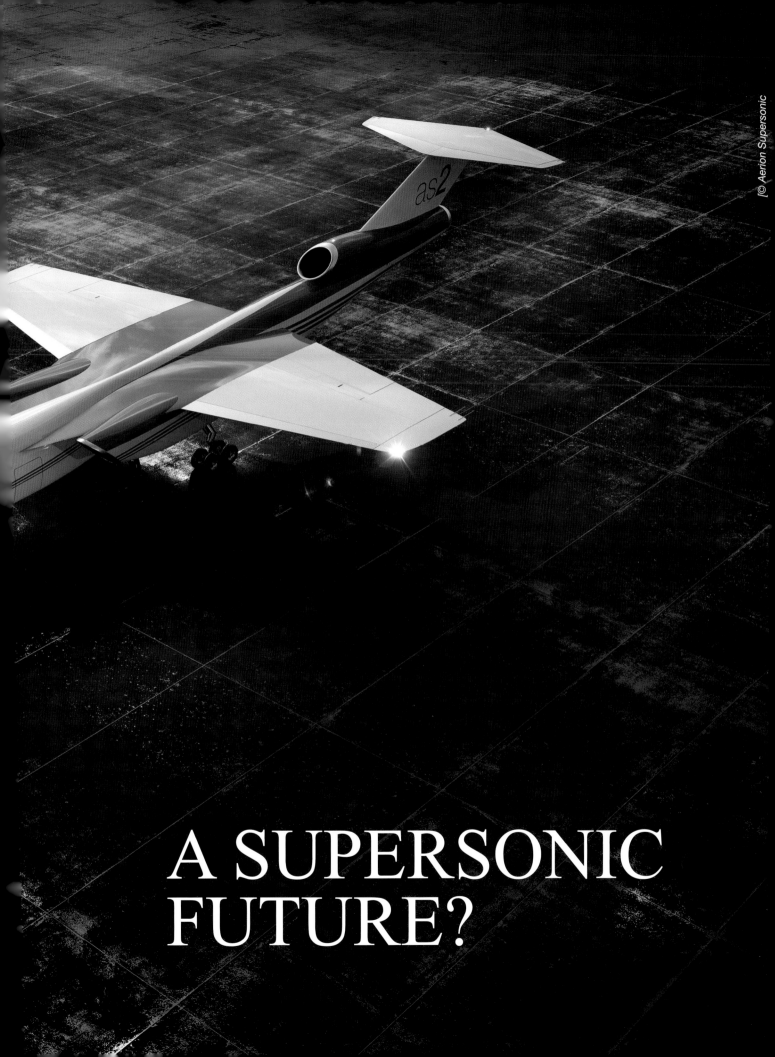

A SUPERSONIC FUTURE?

Since Concorde's retirement in 2003 aviation professionals and enthusiasts alike have been asking one question: Who is going to inherit the crown of 'Queen of the Skies' in the foreseeable future? Besides Concorde's historic rivals – the short-lived Tu-144 and the never completed Boeing 2707 –various ideas and concepts for second-generation supersonic commercial aircraft when Concorde was still in service were being mooted. These ranged from ultrafast business jet designs to long-range airliners with 300 seats. With various concepts being announced, examined, and then either cancelled or shelved, it is difficult to predict the future of supersonic flight. When Concorde was conceived during the late 1950s and early 1960s, her 'fathers' believed that 'speed would sell seats' and that enough passengers would be willing to pay significantly more for their airfare in order to save time when travelling long distances. With the environmental lobby becoming vocal, and fuel prices climbing significantly during the 1970s – thus prompting the world's airlines to cancel their Concorde orders and instead buy the economically more viable Boeing 747 – Concorde entered service in an era far different from when she was conceived fifteen years earlier. Therefore, the prediction, or assumption, that the circumstances for Concorde's success – defined by several hundred orders to cover the enormously high development costs and generate sustained revenue – appeared favourable, was ultimately wrong. From the day when a next-generation supersonic airliner – or any type of aircraft – is conceived, to the day it takes off on its maiden flight, the basis or 'sands' for a successful career might have shifted so dramatically that the concept becomes obsolete. The planners of Concorde's heirs have to be aware that they are working on 'shifting sands', too.

Concorde B

A few months after she had entered commercial service in 1976, Aérospatiale proposed a 'Concorde B', a more refined variant of the existing model. It featured a slightly larger fuel capacity and more powerful and more fuel-efficient Olympus engines without the thirsty and noisy reheat system. Another innovation was the redesigned shape of the delta wing with leading-edge slats that could be drooped like Concorde's nose. The pilot could move them down to improve lift during take-off and landing, and raise them for supersonic flight in order to reduce drag. All these modifications combined would have given Concorde an additional operational range of up to 500 miles (805 km), thus enabling her to be used on new commercial routes including Frankfurt to New York. Although proposed to go into production as the successor of the sixteen completed production Concordes by 1982, this promising project did not become a reality due to the poor sales of the original Concordes and the rising fuel costs of the 1970s.

One of the fourteen production Concordes in service. Concorde B would have featured a redesigned delta wing shape.
[© Air France Museum]

United States

Wind tunnel testing of a Boeing-designed model for a High-Speed Supersonic Commercial Transport (HSCT) in 1993. Its shape resembled the cancelled Boeing 2707.
[© NASA]

Across the Atlantic, after the cancellation of the American SST (Supersonic Transport) programme in 1971, NASA began research on various potential designs for supersonic aircraft. During the late 1980s, after an interruption due to the lack of funding, NASA launched the High-Speed Research (HSR) programme. Partially based on the cancelled Boeing 2707 and supported by the American aviation industry, universities and the government, the project aimed to develop a second-generation supersonic airliner, known as the High-Speed Supersonic Commercial Transport (HSCT) that would be economically feasible, environmentally acceptable and capable of flying over land without creating a sonic boom. With a speed of Mach 2.4 (1,840 mph, 2,960 kph) it was intended to carry 300 passengers across the Atlantic or the Pacific at an affordable price slightly higher than those of subsonic airliners. Unlike Concorde, the HSCT concept had neither a droop nose nor a direct forward view for the pilots. Instead it featured cameras and sensors generating an artificial view (synthetic vision) of the runway on screens inside the cockpit. This system was successfully tested on board various converted airliners during take-offs and landings to prove its feasibility. NASA's HSR research programme also saw the use of existing military aircraft for research, including a delta-winged F-16XL modified with a 'glove' made of titanium.

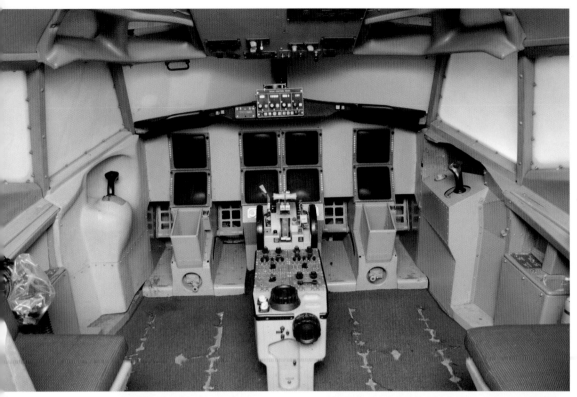

Cockpit of a Boeing 737 used to test the artificial view (synthetic vision) of the runway on screens inside the cockpit.
[© Ted Huetter, Museum of Flight]

The glove contained more than ten million holes and had a suction system attached to the lower surface comprising tubes, valves and a compressor. During research flight the suction systems pulled a small part of the boundary layer of air through the glove's porous surface to create laminar (or smooth) airflow. Researchers believe that laminar flow conditions can reduce aerodynamic drag (friction) and contribute to reduced operating costs by improving fuel consumption and reduction of aircraft weight. By 1999 it was clear that building a prototype seemed possible. However, there were still too many technical, economic, environmental, and manufacturing challenges that needed to be overcome in order to progress to the construction stage of a viable commercial airliner, which, in the end, brought the HSR research programme to an end.

The sonic boom generated by Concorde during her operational service resulted in massive public opposition in the United States and elsewhere, thus preventing Concorde from flying over populated areas in these countries. With this obstacle being a major

The F-16XL with the left wing converted for the experiment to achieve laminar (smooth) airflow by an internal suction system.
[© NASA]

Opposite: Lasers illuminate airflow over a model F-16XL in a NASA wind tunnel.
[© NASA]

In 2003, the 'Shaped Sonic Boom Experiment' (SSBN) between NASA and Northrop Grumman saw the use of a Northrop F-5E with a modified fuselage successfully demonstrating that the aircraft's shock wave, and accompanying sonic boom, which can be shaped, and thereby reduced.
[© Carla Thomas, NASA]

reason for the poor sales of Concorde in the 1970s, a solution to overcome the 'boom problem' has to be found if supersonic air travel is to have a future. Over the years, various proposals for structural modifica-tions to aircraft fuselages to mitigate sonic booms have been made. In 2004, the business jet manufacturer Gulfstream, in cooperation with NASA, approached the issue differently. Their 'Quite Spike' project used a retractable 24-feet-(7.3 m-) long spike which was mounted on a NASA Mc-Donnell Douglas F-15B Eagle research aircraft. During various test flights with a speed of up to Mach 1.8, the spike created three small shock waves travel-ling parallel to each other all the way to the ground, thus producing less noise than typical shock waves that build up at the front of supersonic jets.

NASA's F-15B research testbed with the 'Quiet Spike' attachment, made of composite materials.
[© NASA]

Europe

Not only the US government and some of America's leading aviation manufacturers, most notably represented by NASA, Boeing, and McDonnell Douglas, were interested in further developing SST technology for future civilian commercial use. Aware that Concorde one day would have to be succeeded by a new variant capable of competing with non-European designs, British Aerospace (BAE), the successor of BAC, Aérospatiale, the successor of Sud Aviation, and the Deutsche Aerospace AG (DASA) began their respective research work for new concepts. In 1994, they signed a 'supersonic agreement', resulting in the European Supersonic Research Programme (ESRP), aimed at examining the commercial feasibility of developing a Concorde successor capable of carrying 250 passengers at the speed of Mach 2 over a distance of more than 6,000 miles (10,000 km). Like the American research, the European approach was to meet noise reduction and environmental requirements.

Despite being commercial competitors, it made sense for the ESRP, Boeing, McDonnell Douglas, as well as Italian, Japanese and Russian aviation firms to share their ecological responsibility. Therefore, they were members of an international consortium, called the Supersonic Study Group, which met twice a year to discuss issues such as the environmental impact of future commercial supersonic flight and likely demand. With NASA providing governmental research and funding benefitting the US aircraft manufacturers, so did the German space agency, the Deutsche Zentrum für Luft- und Raumfahrt e.V. (DLR), the British Defence Evaluation and Research Agency (DERA), and the French Office National d'Etudes et de Recherches Aérospatiales (ONERA) supporting the European programme. Conceived as a long-range aircraft, it was to fly across the Atlantic, the Pacific or directly from Europe to Asia with ticket prices not substantially higher than on subsonic airliners. In order to fly over oceans and long overland distances without causing the prohibitive sonic boom, such as the continental United States, the aircraft had to be capable of flying both supersonic and transonic speeds, the latter at Mach 0.95 during the 'land leg' of a flight.

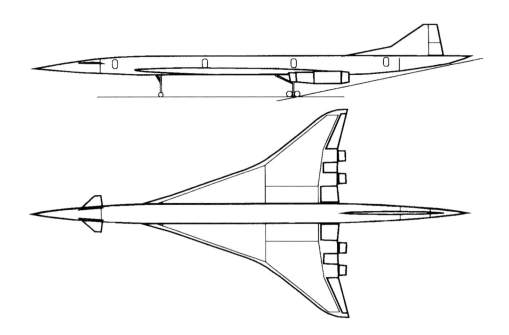

Concorde's successor as conceived by the European Supersonic Research Programme (ESRP) during the 1990s.

Japan

The Japan Aerospace Exploration Agency (JAXA), the Japan Aircraft Development Corporation, and the Society of Japanese Aerospace Companies, also have been working on a successor for Concorde since the late 1980s. Called the 'Next Generation Supersonic Transport', the concept originally aimed for an aircraft capable of carrying 300 passengers at a speed of Mach 2.2 over a distance of 5,500 miles. In the early 2000s this concept was altered to a design with 250 seats with a maximum range of 6,000 miles and a cruising speed of Mach 1.6. Besides the research for a Concorde successor, JAXA has also been working on a concept for a quiet supersonic business jet (SSBJ) for several years.

Supersonic Business Jets – The Next Step?

Although there are currently no supersonic business jets in service, several manufacturers are confident that supersonic travel can be rather achieved with smaller and more cost-effective aircraft than with larger designs struggling to overcome engineering, economic and environmental obstacles. Moreover, the potential 'fathers' of future SSBJs believe that there is a potentially a small yet financially viable target group, such as world leaders or business executives wishing for high-speed air travel. Several established aircraft manufacturers with experience in designing supersonic technology, such as Tupolev with its recently proposed Tu-444, Lockheed or Dassault, and various start-up companies have been working on different SSBN concepts. Among these, the following three concepts, all aiming to be introduced into service during the 2020s, are among the most promising:

Watch Video:

Super-
sonic
Future

Please see instructions on page 2.

Full-scale mockup of the proposed Aerion AS2 supersonic business jet.
[© Aerion Supersonic]

Aerion AS2

The American firm Aerion Supersonic, in cooperation with Lockheed Martin and GE Aviation, is currently developing a twelve-seat SSBJ capable of flying across the Atlantic non-stop and across the Pacific with one stop (in Hawaii) at a speed of Mach 1.4 over sea and Mach 0.95 over land, thus not producing a sonic boom.

The luxurious interior of the Aerion AS2.
[© Aerion Supersonic]

The Aerion AS2 has a range of 4,200 nautical miles (7,780 km) at Mach 1.4 over water or 5,400 nautical miles (10,000 km) at Mach 0.95 over land, although 'boomless' Mach 1.1 flight is possible.
[© Aerion Supersonic]

Spike S-512

The American firm Aerion Supersonic, in cooperation with Lockheed Martin and GE Aviation, is currently developing a twelve-seat SSBJ capable of flying across the Atlantic non-stop and across the Pacific with one stop (in Hawaii) at a speed of Mach 1.4 over sea and Mach 0.95 over land, thus not producing a sonic boom.

The shape of the Spike S-512 shows some resemblance to Concorde.
[© Spike Aerospace / Spike-Aerospace.com]

The Spike S-512 will not have cabin windows, instead it will be lined with tiny cameras sending footage to displays lining the interior walls.
[© Spike Aerospace / Spike-Aerospace.com]

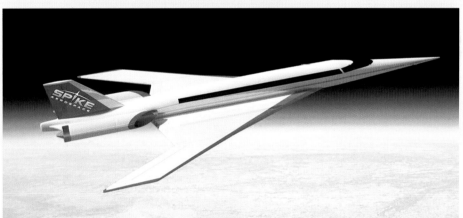

Layout of a conference room in the cabin of the Spike S-512.
[© Spike Aerospace / SpikeAerospace.com]

Boom XB-1 Baby Boom

Another American firm, Boom Aerospace, is currently developing a one-third-scale supersonic testbed and demonstrator aircraft called the XB-1 Baby Boom as the basis for a fifty-five-seat supersonic airliner suitable for transoceanic routes with tickets prices similar to subsonic business class.

Boom Aerospace has entered into a partnership with Virgin Atlantic's The Spaceship Company. Virgin has options for several aircraft as does another unnamed airline. The shape of the proposed airliner suspiciously resembles Concorde's shape conceived more than fifty years earlier.

Boom's supersonic airliner features a refined ogival delta wing with swept trailing edge.

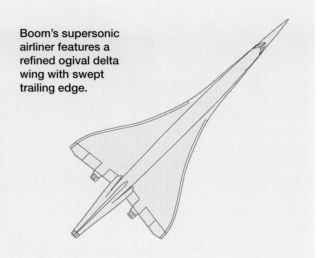

Lockheed Martin X-59 QueSST

The Lockheed Martin X-59 QueSST (Quiet Supersonic Transport) is an experimental supersonic aircraft under development for NASA's 'Low-Boom Flight Demonstrator' programme. With the long nose-cone obstructing the pilots' forward vision, the X-59 will feature an enhanced flight vision system, consisting of a forward camera system compensating for the lack of forward visibility. Propelled by a single General Electric F414 turbofan with reheat, it is intended to reach Mach 1.5 and cruise at Mach 1.42 at 55,000 feet (16,800 m). The X-59's future purpose is to test the feasibility of 'quiet' supersonic technology over urban areas in the United States, in order to overcome a major obstacle for future supersonic air travel.

The X-59 QueSST has been funded by NASA to the tune of $247.5 million.
[© NASA]

Hypersonic Flight – A New Dimension?

With commercial supersonic airliners (Concorde, Tu-144) capable of reaching speeds in excess of Mach 2 and the US Air Force's reconnaissance aircraft Lockheed SR-71 Blackbird capable of Mach 3.3 (retired in 1999), aircraft engineers are now looking at even faster designs to carry passengers around the world. Among several proposed concepts are conventional turbojet and ramjet designs capable of flying at speeds in excess of Mach 5 (3,850 mph, 6,200 kph). Even faster designs, however, would call for rocket or scramjet propulsion systems.

Hypersonic Flight

Hypersonic speed is one that can be described as highly supersonic, generally referring to speeds of Mach 5 and higher. A ramjet is a form of an air-breathing jet engine using the engine's forward motion for compressing the incoming air without the use of an axial compressor or a centrifugal compressor. Ramjets cannot move an aircraft from a standstill as they cannot produce thrust at zero speed. Therefore, a ramjet-powered vehicle requires an assisted take-off like an aircraft ('mother ship') or a rocket assist to accelerate it to a speed where it can begin to produce thrust itself.

Reaction Engines A2

The British aerospace firm Reaction Engines Limited is currently working on a design study called the LAPCAT A2 for an environmentally friendly, long-range, hypersonic airliner. The aircraft was originally part of the LAPCAT programme (Long-Term Advanced Propulsion Concepts and Technologies), co-funded by the European Union. With a range of 12,000 miles (20,000 km) and capable of a top speed of more than Mach 5, the LAPCAT A2 is intended to carry 300 passengers from Europe to Australia in about 4.6 hours at a height of 100,000 feet (30 km) in the 2040s, compared to a complete travelling day on a present-day subsonic aircraft. The four Scimitar engines, originally conceived for space launch but modifiable for intercontinental high-speed air travel, will use liquid hydrogen as a fuel having twice the specific impulse of kerosene, and can be used to cool the vehicle and the air entering the engines via a pre-cooler. The ticket cost is aimed at business-class level.

SonicStar and HyperStar

In 2008, the US-based HyperMach Aerospace Industries, Inc. was formed to design a twin-engine hypersonic business jet capable of carrying about twenty passengers at Mach 3.6 over a distance of 6,000 nautical miles (11,000 km). Later renamed Hyperstar, the aircraft concept performance was improved to a speed of Mach 5 at 80,000 feet, an increased range of 7,000 nautical miles and a larger passenger capacity of up to thirty-six passengers. The firm is experimenting with a system called the electromagnetic drag-reduction technology (EDRT) that will mitigate, and possibly even eliminate, the sonic boom, thus enabling the Hyperstar to fly over land.

199

ZEHST

Presented in 2011 the Zero Emission Hyper Sonic Transport (ZEHST) is a future airliner concept envisioned by Airbus in cooperation with the Japan Aerospace Exploration Agency (JAXA). It is intended to carry up to a hundred passengers at a speed of Mach 4 at a height of 100,000 feet, thus being capable of flying from Europe to Japan in 2.5 hours or from London to New York in just one hour. Propelled by biofuel made from seaweed and by oxygen/hydrogen, it is to consist of three propulsion systems: two turbofans to be used for take-off and reaching Mach 0.8, then rocket boosters to take over to accelerate to Mach 2.5, then two scramjets to enable the ZEHST to reach its cruising speed of Mach 4. Airbus envisions the aircraft to fly by 2050.

SpaceLiner

Conceived by the Deutsche Zentrum für Luft- und Raumfahrt, Germany's space agency, the Space-Liner is a concept for hypersonic transport. Besides carrying passengers it is also intended to be used as a reusable launch vehicle (RLV) capable of delivering heavy payloads into orbit. Propelled by a single type of reusable rocket engine, liquid hydrogen and liquid oxygen will be used as the propellants, a combination that is both very powerful and environmentally friendly. Conceived as a long-term project, the SpaceLiner might become operational during the 2040s.

Artist's impression of the SpaceLiner 7 during the ascent phase.
[© Deutsches Zentrum für Luft- und Raumfahrt / DLR]

Artist's impression of the SpaceLiner 7 at the moment of booster separation.
[© Deutsches Zentrum für Luft- und Raumfahrt / DLR]

Boeing Hypersonic Airliner

In 2018, Boeing presented its concept for a future Mach 5 hypersonic jet capable of crossing the Atlantic in two and the Pacific in three hours, thus enabling the airlines to use it for same-day return flights and thereby increasing the aircraft's profitability. Larger than business jets, it would be powered by a turboramjet which is a hybrid engine that essentially consists of a turbojet mounted inside a ramjet. The turboramjet can be run in turbojet mode at take-off and during low-speed flight but can then switch to ramjet mode to enable the aircraft to accelerate to Mach 5. With this engine concept working without the use of reheat, it would cause less noise during take-off. Made of titanium, the hypersonic airliner is intended to become operational during the 2020s. The project benefits from the experience gained from the tests with the Boeing X-51 Waverider which is an unmanned research scramjet experimental aircraft used for hypersonic flight at Mach 5.

With most of the concepts currently under development and intended to take to the skies between the 2020s and 2040s as testbeds, demonstrators or for commercial service, it is difficult to predict which of these eventually will establish itself. However, the contenders for the second generation of commercial supersonic air travel have to be economically viable, environmentally acceptable and capable of flying over land without creating a disturbing sonic boom. Therefore, we will need to keep a watchful eye for a new aircraft that one day might inherit the crown of 'Queen of the Skies' from the dignified Concorde.

The X-51A Waverider, shown here under the wing of a B-52 Stratofortress, was used to demonstrate hypersonic flight.
[© U.S. Air Force]

SIGNIFICANCE
AND LEGACY
OF CONCORDE

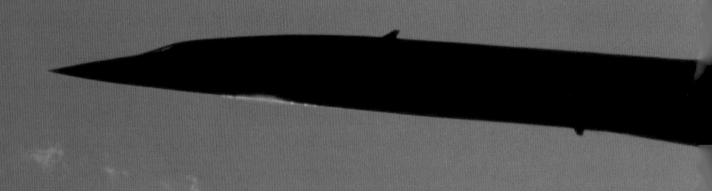

*"We should remember Concorde by telling the
story of the human spirit she represents."*

— Pierre Grange, former AF Concorde pilot

Concorde has different meanings to different people as everyone has developed an individual – and often very personal – connection to her. Her unique and flamboyant career has captured the imagination of people from around the world, including Concorde professionals, passengers, and enthusiasts alike. They all share a common bond – a timeless adoration for this technological marvel and design icon. In their own words, they describe Concorde's unique charisma, and her legacy:

"For me, Concorde is the emblematic icon of an era, the 1960s. This was the last era in our history when the spirit of conquest still reigned. At that time, the Americans embarked on their journey to the moon and we built Concorde. In France and Great Britain, decision-makers gave an exceptional generation the opportunity to meet the exceptional challenges posed by supersonic transport and they did it brilliantly. Concorde enabled the emergence and success of Airbus, thus allowing the creation of the industrial fabric necessary for major aeronautical programmes. To this day, Concorde remains as a symbol of European know-how. In France, we think of her as a French aircraft, although British know how, especially on gine technology, was vital. Nevertheless, the French are very proud of Concorde. We should remember her by telling the story of the human spirit she represents, and this is the mission of APCOS (Association des professionnels de Concorde et du supersonique), the association of former Concorde professionals, whose chairman I am. APCOS honours the commitment and enthusiasm of all those who made Concorde fly."

– Pierre Grange, former AF Concorde pilot

"Concorde Fox Alpha (F-BVFA) is one of our most popular artefacts and highlights the capabilities of aeronautical technology from the 1960s. Despite the fact that she was not a commercial success, Concorde still captures the public's imagination because of her grace and beauty. Her legacy is, perhaps, to make sure that the technological possibilities match the economic realities when designing commercial aircraft. As technologically advanced as Concorde was, she could not make money and ultimately, that is the purpose of an airliner."

– Robert van der Linden, Smithsonian Institution

"In the 1960s and 1970s, Concorde was such a powerful symbol that even those who could not afford to buy a ticket, had taken up their own means of ownership of Concorde.

Fox Fox (F-BVFF) preserved at the Charles de Gaulle Airport.
[© Vicentiu Ciorlaus]

She showed that major projects could motivate an entire country and made those who participated proud."

– Philippe Gebarowski, French Concorde passenger

"I think Concorde encapsulated so many aspects of a lifestyle the majority of the world could only dream about. My time on Concorde taught me what true service is and how every detail matters to ensure that you are delivering a flawless experience. For Britain, she was the jewel in the crown."

– Iona Ferguson, former BA Concorde flight attendant

"There is no aircraft today – civilian or military – that compares to Concorde, that can fly that fast, that far, that high and with that load, all in shirt-sleeve comfort. She showed that France and Britain could solve difficult problems that the rest of the world could not. The Americans tried, but finished up with a wooden mock-up. The Russians tried but proved that their technology was not up to the challenge

and gave up after very few flights. The late English engineer Barnes Wallis summed the situation up well when he compared the British approach with that of the American: 'America threw money at the project, the United Kingdom threw brains at it. In the end, brains will always win.'"

– Ian Kirby, former BA Concorde flight engineer

"Concorde's charisma was her look, both on the ground and in flight. She is an exceptional and majestic aircraft as a result of the cooperation between two countries. The same goal and a team spirit shared by everyone involved in this project made this aircraft become a reality."

– Patrick Sevestre, former AF Concorde ground engineer

"Concorde attracted many famous personalities and this added to her general ethos: passengers talked about their flight experiences and still remember them today. Concorde was easy on the eye and quite distinctive from other aircraft. The small size of

the fleet also added to the remarkable character that is Concorde."

– Philip Cairns, former BA ground engineer

"Concorde was more than the parts she was made from – she was a symphony of extreme engineering, human spirit, renowned service and sheer beauty. I truly don't think anything can ever replace her and have the same 'soul' that she had. But Concorde will always live on through museums, videos and books like this, hopefully inspiring generations to come."

– Johnathan Safford, American Concorde passenger

"Concorde is something to be justifiably proud of, illustrating just what can be achieved in life if you have the right people in the right place at the right time. Concorde defined my career in aviation, and even brought my lovely wife Liz and me together."

– Ricky Bastin, former BA ground engineer

"Concorde is an ambassador of Anglo-French technology and intelligence, enormously admired by the whole world. She is a jewel we loved to show to the world. I still remember our last Concorde around-the-world tour in 2000 which included three of my colleagues who died a few months later in the tragic Concorde accident in Paris. To this day, I still receive letters from passengers who were on this tour, making me recall all these precious moments we were lucky enough to share."

– Alain Verschuere, former AF Concorde purser

"Concorde still to this day inspires young people who have never seen Concorde. I talk to a lot of young people in lectures and meet young training engineers who all find Concorde inspirational. Concorde should be remembered with great affection and very happy memories. She is beautiful, she is inspirational. She was slightly demanding like any very beautiful woman."

– John Hutchinson, former BA Concorde captain

The Legacy of Concorde

by Katie John, editor of *Mach 2* magazine

On 26 November 2003 British Airways Concorde Alpha Fox (G-BOAF) settled to earth for the last time, bringing to an end the first era of supersonic air travel. Concorde began as a dream of the next advance in human technology; then the cost of its development and operation rendered the aircraft a luxury for the elite, or for those who saved up for a trip of a lifetime. Now the fleets have retired to museums, apparently to become just an interesting byway in the history of flight.

Lingering Influence

The prevailing view of Concorde seems to be that she was technically spectacular but a giant waste of money and effort. Yet Concorde influenced aviation profoundly, in ways that are perhaps not generally recognized. The most notable example is the fly-by-wire system; Concorde was the first airliner to use such a system. Another example is the use of lightweight carbon brakes; this innovation, in the early 1970s, was then adopted for Formula 1 racing cars and later for other passenger aircraft. Further to the development seen in the aircraft itself, the detailed airworthiness standards that the British and French had to develop in order to operate Concorde formed the basis for the pan-European Joint Airworthiness Requirements (JARs), which have evolved further into today's European Aviation Safety Agency (EASA) standards. Lastly, in the words of one former site manager at Toulouse, Concorde "trained a whole generation of shop floor workers, engineers, and managers" who would go on to build the mighty Airbus company.

An Enduring Icon

Concorde was the creation of high politics and the instrument of big business. Yet for fifty years, from the moment the prototypes first appeared, the aircraft has won admiration from people around the world. Among Europe's grands projects, Concorde stands alone in winning this spontaneous love from so many people. Spectators thrilled to the sight of the aircraft at air shows and on national occasions in the UK and France. During the autumn of 2003, crowds gathered at airports to watch the final flights. And still today, Concorde is as popular as ever.

Thousands of people visit the aircraft on display in museums. Even more people talk, argue, rhapsodise, and share memories about the beautiful white bird. Concorde is enjoying a second life in cyberspace, with internet groups attracting passionate followers, and new videos of Concorde in flight appearing every day. Former Concorde pilots and engineers give talks to full houses. Even in casual conversation, people often ask why Concorde stopped flying or whether she could be returned to flight. Most recently, in the last few years, former Concorde personnel and volunteers at a few of the museums have brought their Concordes partially back to life. Flight deck controls light up, and navigation lights flash. In a couple of cases, hydraulic power has been supplied so that the famous nose moves up and down. Direct experience of the aircraft is being maintained and passed on to others – so, until the next supersonic airliners appear, for Concorde it is not goodbye but simply *au revoir*.

Alpha Delta (G-BOAD) preserved at the Intrepid Sea-Air-Space Museum, New York. [© *Jean-Philippe Lemaire*]

Concorde Details by Name

Number: 001	Registration: F-WTSS	First Flight: 2 March 1969	Last Flight: 19 October 1973	Hours Flown: 812

French prototype. Roll-out on 11 December 1967. First supersonic flight on 1 October 1969, first Mach 2 flight on 4 November 1970. Total of 397 flights including 249 at supersonic speed. Preserved at the Air & Space Museum, Le Bourget, near Paris, France.

Number: 002	Registration: G-BBST	First Flight: 9 April 1969	Last Flight: 4 March 1976	Hours Flown: 836

British prototype. Roll-out on 19 September 1968. First supersonic flight on 25 March 1970, first Mach 2 flight on 12 November 1970. Total of 438 flights including 196 at supersonic speed. Preserved at the Fleet Air Arm Museum, Yeovilton, England.

Number: 101	Registration: G-AXDN	First Flight: 17 December 1971	Last Flight: 20 August 1977	Hours Flown: 632

British pre-production Concorde. Differences to prototypes included modified wings and engines, and larger fuel tanks. Reached the fasted speed of any Concorde by flying at Mach 2.23. Preserved at the Imperial War Museum, Duxford, England.

Number: 102	Registration: F-WTSA	First Flight: 10 January 1973	Last Flight: 20 May 1976	Hours Flown: 656

French pre-production Concorde. First one built in the final shape of the production Concordes. First one to visit the US. Wore AF livery on one side and BA on the other. Used as a source of spare parts for AF Concordes after retirement. Preserved at the Musée Delta, Orly Airport, Paris, France.

Number: 201	Registration: F-WTSB	First Flight: 6 December 1973	Last Flight: 19 April 1985	Hours Flown: 909

French production test aircraft. Although considered a production aircraft, never entered commercial service. Preserved at the Aeroscopia Museum at Toulouse, France.

Number: 202	Registration: G-BBDG	First Flight: 13 December 1974	Last Flight: 24 December 1981	Hours Flown: 1,282

British production test aircraft. Although considered a production aircraft, 201 never entered commercial airline service. The first one to carry 100 passengers at Mach 2. Used as a source of spare parts. Refurbished, restored, and preserved at the Brooklands Museum, Weybridge, England.

Number: 203	Registration: F-BTSC	First Flight: 31 January 1975	Last Flight: 25 July 2000	Hours Flown: 11,989

Built as a production test aircraft (F-WTSC). Re-registered as F-BTSC in 1975 for AF service. Out of service from 1980-1986, it carried Pope John Paul II to Africa in 1989. Destroyed in a crash after take-off from Paris CDG on 25 July 2000, killing 113 people.

Number: 204	Registration: G-BOAC	First Flight: 27 February 1975	Last Flight: 31 October 2003	Hours Flown: 22,260

First used on the Bahrain/Singapore routes, 1976. Re-registered as G-N81AC/N81AC for service with Braniff Airways in 1979. Re-registered as G-BOAC in 1980 after discontinuation of the Braniff service. Preserved at the Manchester Airport Viewing Park, England.

Number: 205	Registration: F-BVFA	First Flight: 27 October 1975	Last Flight: 12 June 2003	Hours Flown: 17,824

Flew the first AF flight to Rio de Janeiro via Dakar on 21 Jan. 1976. Re-registered as N94FA for Braniff Airways service, 1979. Registered as F-BVFA, 1980. Flew around the world in a record-breaking 41 hours 27 minutes, 1988. Preserved at the Nat. Air & Space Museum, Wash., D.C.

Number: 206	Registration: G-BOAA	First Flight: 5 November 1975	Last Flight: 12 August 2000	Hours Flown: 22,768

Flew the first BA flight to Bahrain on 21 Jan. 1976. Re-registered as G-N49AA/N49AA for Braniff service, 1979. Re-registered as G-BOAA, 1980. Was not fitted with the safety modifications required after the 2000 crash and hence retired. Preserved at the Nat. Museum of Flight, Scotland.

Number: 207	Registration: F-BVFB	First Flight: 6 March 1976	Last Flight: 24 June 2003	Hours Flown: 14,771

Re-registered as N94FB for Braniff service, 1979. Re-registered as F-BVFB, 1980. Out of service from 1990-1997. Preserved at the Technik Museum Sinsheim, Germany.

Number: 208	Registration: G-BOAB	First Flight: 18 May 1976	Last Flight: 15 August 2000	Hours Flown: 22,296

Re-registered as G-N94AB/N94AB for Braniff service, 1979. Re-registered as G-BOAB, 1980. When Concorde returned to service after the crash, BA only required five aircraft. Therefore, it was not fitted with the safety modifications and hence retired. Currently in storage at Heathrow Airport.

Number: 209	Registration: F-BVFC	First Flight: 9 July 1976	Last Flight: 27 June 2003	Hours Flown: 14,332

Re-registered as N94FC for service with Braniff Airways, 1979. Re-registered as F-BVFC, 1980. Preserved at the Aeroscopia Museum near Airbus Factory at Toulouse, France.

Number: 210	Registration: G-BOAD	First Flight: 25 August 1976	Last Flight: 10 November 2003	Hours Flown: 23,397

Was the only BA Concorde wearing the BA livery on one side and the Singapore Airl. livery on the other, 1979. Re-registered as G-N94AD/N94AD for Braniff service, 1979. Re-registered as G-BOAD, 1980. Preserved at the Intrepid Sea-Air-Space Museum, New York, USA.

Number: 211	Registration: F-BVFD	First Flight: 10 February 1977	Last Flight: 27 May 1982	Hours Flown: 5,814

Re-registered as N94FD for Braniff service, 1979. Re-registered as F-BVFD, 1980. Retired after the discontinuation of the AF route to Dakar/Rio. Used as a source of spare parts and badly corroded after being stored outdoors. Broken up in 1994. Fuselage sections in storage.

Number: 212	Registration: G-BOAE	First Flight: 17 March 1977	Last Flight: 17 November 2003	Hours Flown: 23,376

Re-registered as G-N94AE/N94AE for Braniff service, 1979. Re-registered as G-BOAE, 1980. Flew in formation with the Red Arrows to mark the opening of the Scottish Parliament, 1999. Preserved at the Grantley Adams Int. Airport, Barbados.

Number: 213	Registration: F-BTSD	First Flight: 26 June 1978	Last Flight: 14 June 2003	Hours Flown: 12,974

Re-registered as N94SD for Braniff service, 1979. Re-registered as F-BTSD, 1980. Holds the world record for flying around the world in both directions. Carried a promotional paint scheme for Pepsi in 1996. Preserved at the Air & Space Museum, Le Bourget, France.

Number: 214	Registration: G-BOAG	First Flight: 21 April 1978	Last Flight: 5 November 2003	Hours Flown: 16,239

Originally registered as G-BFKW to BAE in 1978 but later sold to BA and re-registered as G-BOAG. Used as a source of spares during the early 1980s. Restored to flying condition using parts from Air France – F-BVFD in 1984. Preserved at the Museum of Flight, Seattle, USA.

Number: 215	Registration: F-BVFF	First Flight: 26 December 1978	Last Flight: 11 June 2000	Hours Flown: 12,421

Originally registered as F-WJAN to Aérospatiale, re-registered to AF as F-BVFF, 1980. Retired in 2000 to be used as a source of spare parts for F-BTSD. In the process of being restored to flying condition when AF retired its fleet. Preserved at the CDG Airport, Paris, France.

Number: 216	Registration: G-BOAF	First Flight: 20 April 1979	Last Flight: 26 November 2003	Hours Flown: 18,257

Last Concorde to be built. Originally registered as G-BFKX to BAE in 1978, then loaned to Braniff (G-N94AF) and BA (G-BOAF). Finally sold to BA in 1980. Last Concorde ever to fly from Heathrow to Filton, on 26 November 2003. Preserved at Aerospace Bristol, England.

Concorde Facts	(Source: British Airways)
Capacity	100 passengers and 2.5 tonnes of cargo
Seating	100 seats, 40 in the front cabin and 60 in the rear cabin
Range	4,143 miles (6,667 km)
Engines	Four Rolls-Royce/SNECMA Olympus 593s, each producing 38,000lb of thrust with reheat
Take-off speed	250 mph (400 kph)
Cruising speed	1,350 mph (2,160 kph/Mach 2) up to 60,000 ft
Landing speed	187mph (300kph)
Length	203ft 9in (62.1m)
Wing span	83ft 8in (25.5 m)
Height	37ft 1in (11.3 m)
Fuselage width	9ft 6in (2.9 m)
Fuel capacity	26,286 Imperial gallons (119,500 litres)
Fuel consumption	5,638 Imperial gallons (25,629 litres) per hour
Maximum take-off weight	408,000 lb (185 tonnes)
Landing gear	Eight main wheels, two nose wheels
Flight crew	Two pilots, one flight engineer
Cabin crew	Six

Sources

Gordon, Yefim; Rigmant, Vladimir (2005). *Tupolev Tu-144*. Hinckley, Leicestershire, UK: Midland.
Orlebar, Christopher (2004). *The Concorde Story*. Oxford, UK: Osprey Publishing.

Personal and telephone interviews (incl. correspondence):
John Hutchinson, Pierre Grange, Gérard Duval, Béatrice Vialle, Ian Kirby, Ricky Bastin, Suzanne O'Donoghue, Iona Ferguson, Annick and Claude Moyal, Katie John and Nigel Ferris (*Mach 2* magazine), Caroline Cadier, Ian Dick, Richard Thomas, Alain Verschuere

Websites:
http://mach-2-magazine.co.uk (retrieved on 6 June 2018)
http://company.airbus.com/company/heritage/now-and-then/concorde.html (retrieved on 12 July 2018)

Photo credits (Supersonic Star Gazing):
J. Callaghan: US NARA; V. G. d'Estaing: Bundesarchiv (BA), B 145 Bild-F056912-0010 / Gräfingholt, Detlef / CC-BY-SA 3.0; Pope John Paul II: BA, B 145 Bild-F059404-0019 / Schaack, Lothar / CC-BY-SA; J. Chirac: US NARA; E. Heath: US DoD; G. Pompidou / H. Wilson: Nationaal Archief LN / Anefo; F. Mitterrand: US DoD; M. Thatcher: US LoC; H. Kissinger: US Dept of State; T. Blair: US NARA; Pr. Margaret: Nationaal Archief NL / Anefo; Pr. Charles: Queensland State Archive; Pr. Andrew: A. Meredith; D. Frost / E. Taylor: US DoD; S. Connery / R. Moore: Nationaal Archief NL; M. Jackson: US NARA; G. Michael: University of Houston; M. Jagger / P. McCartney: Nationaal Archief NL / Anefo; Joan Collins: A. Meredith; C. Eastwood: NASA